CAPITOL
OF
MARYLAND

CAPITOL OF MARYLAND

Jerome Otto Waters, Jr.

Library of Congress Control Number: 2012916535
ISBN: Hardcover   978-1-4771-4394-0
                 Softcover   978-1-4771-4393-3
                 Ebook   978-1-4771-4395-7

To order additional copies of this book, contact:
Xlibris Corporation
1-888-795-4274
www.Xlibris.com
Orders@Xlibris.com
114780

CONTENTS

Acknowledgements...7

Introduction 9

Chapter 1. 101 Lombard Federal Custody........................13

Chapter 2. Supermax...15

Chapter 3. History..19

Chapter 4. The Past—1979......................................20

Chapter 5. The Country...24

Chapter 6. Managing Money 28

Chapter 7. Supermax-Present 30

Chapter 8. Annapolis Woods 31

Chapter 9. Admiral Oaks 33

Chapter 10. Supermax Present 2005 35

Chapter 11. Eastport...37

Chapter 12. Allens Apartments....................................44

Chapter 13. Blood Sweat and Tears 45

Chapter 14. Juvenile Criminal System............................47

Chapter 15. Shelton Ham Juvenile Facility......................51

Chapter 16. The Only People That Seem Perfect at What
            They Do are Gods and Dead People...................55

Chapter 17. The Cook-Up..58

Chapter 18. Higher Learning......................................61

Chapter 19. The Route 63

Chapter 20. The Road to Success.................................73

Chapter 21. Against All Odds......................................80

Chapter 22. If Your Not Part of The Solution, Your Part of
            The Problem 89

Chapter 23. Jessup State Correctional Facility 93

Chapter 24. Present 98

Chapter 25. Product of My Environment..........................100

Chapter 26. The Connect..110

Chapter 27. Annapolis Harbor 114
Chapter 28. "Paid in Full" 117
Chapter 29. Reality 121
Chapter 30. Business as Usual 128
Chapter 31. Present 131
Chapter 32. Living 134
Chapter 33. M.C.I.J. 138
Chapter 34. "Get It How You Live" 142
Chapter 35. Million Dollar Dreams and Federal Nightmares 146
Chapter 36. It Comes With The Game 150
Chapter 37. The Close's Distance Between Two People Is
            Communication 155
Chapter 38. Victory Lap 158
Chapter 39. Game Over 164
Chapter 40. 101 Lombard 167
Chapter 41. Supermax Present 170
Chapter 42. American Justice 181
Chapter 43. The Penitentiary–Adapt or Die 191
Chapter 44. Fairton, Jersey 208
Chapter 45. Adding Insult To Injury 221
About The Author 225

ACKNOWLEDGEMENTS

First, I would like to thank God because without him none of this would be possible. I would like to thank my parents, kids, brother and sisters for sticking by me through thick and thin. I would like to thank all the family members, as well, that have been there by my side from the beginning and still stand by me.

Special Thanks: To my Grandparents, who always showed me unconditional love. Last but not least, I would like to thank those who supported me and encouraged me to write and finish my book: Baltimore's own "Rudy Williams", Maurice "Peanut" King, and my editor Leroy Mckenzie Jr.

INTRODUCTION

The United States does not provide a level playing field for all children and it does not protect all young lives "equally".

Poor children and children of color in particular, already are in the pipeline to prison before taking a single step or uttering a single word.

Much of the problem is due to poverty, and children of color are more likely to be affected. One quarter of Latino children and one-third of African American children grow up poor. African American children are more than three times as likely as Caucasian children to be born into poverty, and are more than four times as likely to live in extreme poverty.

Millions of poor children are failed by their families, the juvenile justice system, and by "child welfare" (reversed) "farewell child". Prison is the only university guaranteed program for children in America. Our country has 2.3 million prisoners, which is the world's largest inmate population. We have more prisoners then China, a nation that has four times as many people as the United States. Those who are incarcerated are disproportionately people of color who are products of a society that has neglected and marginalized them.

Children of color are more likely to be placed in programs for mental retardation and in foster care, and are more likely to be suspended from school, left back a grade, or drop out. A black boy born in 2001 has a one in three chance of going to prison. The reason for this fact is because of unfair drug laws, draconian sentencing, failing schools and a lack of opportunity. There are 580,000 incarcerated black men, many of them are fathers who are doing time in state and federal prisons, while they're only 40,000 who graduate from college each year, so, "crime does pay", one way or another. It's the payout that you're looking for or the payment that you don't want. You'll either behind bars paying your debt to society, or you paid your debt with your life for the crime/crimes that you committed. All of this stems from a lack of commitment by our societies misplaced priorities and squandered resources.

[One in every three black males is involved in the penal system. Blacks make up 13% of the United States population, but make up 50% of those who are waiting on DEATH ROW.[Prosecutors seek the death penalty 70% of the time when a black person kills a white person, but only 19% of the time when the situation is reversed. It's clear that society does not want us to reproduce ourselves. In addition, the government sets up "free clinics" and gives out free birth control pills in the black communities but not in others. Since 1993 legalized abortions have killed more African Americans than AIDS, Black on black violent crimes, heart disease and diabetes combined. 40% of the abortions in this country are made by our most valuable resources, "the black woman". Black leaders today call it "womb lynching". Blacks comprise 17% of the drivers on the "Maryland" state highways, but 70% of those drivers are stopped by police.

[More than 2,300 Maryland inmates were serving a life sentence in 2008. Nearly 77% of those inmates are African Americans, making Maryland the state with the largest share of black prisoners serving life sentences.[Among the 269 prisoners in Maryland sentenced to life for crimes committed when they were juveniles, 226 are black. The only thing "Mary" about this land was "bloody Mary", but don't get it confused with the alcoholic beverage, "Maryland-Murdaland".

In 1982 100,000 black males were incarcerated, today there are 1.3 million. Two out of three blacks were projected to be involved with the drug game, a.k.a. "The Game"

GAME-(noun) **a line of work: profession**
     (verb) **to play for a stake: to take dishonest advantage of**.

100% of the drug games activity in this country revolves around the "American dollar", the **MONEY** is the motive. It's true when they say that the **LOVE OF** money is the root of all evil.

In the early days people had no system of money as we know it today. To get things they wanted, people used the "barter system" (accepting certain goods in exchange for a product or service). The barter system is still used today in the "drug game". Dealers would pay drug addicts for stolen goods or to do services for them in exchange for drugs. Even if you weren't an addict, females would have sex with a person in exchange for that person to pay their bills, get their hair done, etc . . . Even in Corporate America, an employee would have sex with their boss in exchange for a promotion to a higher position, or have special privileges at the work place.

✱ [In 1652, Massachusetts Bay Colony became the first colony to make coins. Massachusetts was also the first colony to produce paper money. In 1690, colonial government issued notes called "bill of credits". The bills were receipts for loans made by citizens to the colonial government, from then on it became money as we know it today.

Only God knows what the Massachusettians knew about the drugs, jealousy, and envy that their discovery would bring to this so called "greatest country on Earth".

For the love of money people would kill and do the strangest things just to have a slice of the "devils Pie".

"My country tears of thee, land of the liberty, aw thee I sing". "Freedom ain't free" in America. It costs more to be free then for you to do life in the penitentiary." "Taxation without Representation". The U.S. government is the worlds largest debtor, **C**ash **R**ules **E**verything **A**round **M**e. For most blacks growing up in poverty and extreme poverty, "the drug game" was the only way they could eat. The Europeans came over to this country and took this land from the Indians and called it "Thanksgiving". In other words "Thanks for giving". In addition, they kidnapped our ancestors and brought them to this land and made them work as slaves, and they expect us to "let freedom ring".

Nigger vs. Nigga

Nigger—Disrespecting and offensive. A member of any dark-skinned people. A member of a people of disadvantaged social standing; second-class citizen. In addition, the "er" on the end of the word "nigger" represents the lynching, whipping, raping, etc . . . of slaves for over 400 years. It also stands for the discrimination, prejudice, and racism that still remains in this country today.

Nigga—a word mostly used by African Americans as a slang. In addition, the "a" on the end of the word "nigga" represents the kidnapping, whipping, raping, etc . . . . Our ancestors were slaves for over 400 years and still managed to survive it. It also stands for the survival of the struggles over the centuries and still in life today, while being black in America.

Nigger in slavery days was what our ancestors were called with a noose around their neck hanging from a tree. Nigga is what we call each other today with gold, platinum, and diamond chains around our necks hanging out in clubs.

C h a p t e r 1

101 Lombard Federal Custody

2005–Present

After the judge banged the gavel, I looked toward the back of the courtroom to see the expression on my family members faces, knowing that I was just denied my return home on house arrest, until my trial started. On the same day of the 9th anniversary of Tupac Shakur's death, I was standing in a federal court house watching my life flash before my eyes. Here I am 5'ft 6" inches tall, dreadlocks in my hair, mad as shit. My mother was looking like someone had just killed her son, knowing that the system had as of 1998 when the judge banged the gavel, after giving her son a 5 year sentence, in a state prison. She tried to hold back tears, but was unable to do so. It was a dark and cold day for her at the Annapolis Circuit Court House. She never turned her back on neither of her sons, and wasn't planning on doing so now. Déjà Vue all over again! She remembered back when she used to go through the same situation with his father, when she was a teenager. It scares her so much hoping that her son doesn't end up like him. She can still feel the hurt and pain that his father caused her, like it was yesterday. You would've never thought that the last time they had been in a relationship was over 20 years ago.

The disappointing look on Mr. Walder's mother's face let the $75,000 lawyer know that her and the rest of his clients supporters that day, was blind toward the federal laws. "Conspiracy" was a mean and hateful word throughout the federal system. It was the one charge that had 90% of blacks locked up with the feds. A charge that was easy to catch, but hard to beat.

Larry said, "Ms. Joan . . . I'm a take care of everything. Your son will be transferred to the "supermax" until his trial, which could take about a year . . . the only evidence that the feds have is 15-20 people that's willing to testify against him for the prosecutor, if they're needed".

It was hard for Ms. Joan to put her son's life in the hands of a white man. Through her whole life the white man was the main person who sent every male who she loved away, including her father when she was only 6 years old.

My family all looked as if they were at my funeral instead of my initial appearance. "The Big Boys", is what we called the feds in Annapolis because they were considered over all law enforcement. Everybody who I knew that went to the feds got a life sentence or basketball #'s that was represented by months.

I was so mad at the judge's decision that I forgot about my co–defendants who were beside me with their families in the back of the court room going through the same emotions as my family was.

As the marshal guided me out of the court room, I looked at my family and assured them that I'll call home later on that day.

The bullpin at 101 Lombard had the smell of shit from scared and nervous inmates letting out their last bowel movement before the judge decided their sentence. The bag lunches the marshal gave us wasn't any help either, it was just letting us know that we wouldn't be eating back at the "supermax". The speakers outside the cages were used to further incriminate the stupid inmates that couldn't keep their mouths shut.

C h a p t e r   2

Supermax

A t the supermax, Howell and I later learned that our co-defendant, who was in court with us, was awarded house arrest.

The C.O.'s put us in the bullpen with about 10 other inmates. The sergeant, who looked like a taller "flava flav", told us all to strip ass naked and throw our clothes in the hallway. One by one he watched us bend over, squat and cough. After we finished, he gave us a burgundy uniform and a laundry bag with supermax supplies inside.

A voice yelled out "Howell . . . Howell!" I looked at my cousin, he looked at me and yelled back "yeah!" A short woman about 5 feet tall came walking down to the bullpen. Her name was "Ms. Rien". She was good people's to all the federal inmates, even though she worked for the government, she knew that they were locking niggas up for no reason at all. She looked at my cousin and said, "Damn boy, you look just like your father . . . your father will be back at the "max" in a couple of weeks". My cousin said, "ok".

After everybody in the bullpin was in their uniform, the sergeant walked us through the hallway up to the second floor. My cousin and I shared a cell together on block F-2. Back in the cell I told him that his boy "low" wasn't right back in 2003 when one of my Eastport comrade's told me that he got a nigga locked up by telling on him about a gun situation, he wouldn't listen though.

The supermax was a concrete jungle filled with murderers, predators, drug distributors and gangstaz. If you was over the supermax federal custody, that meant that the feds wanted you and that you were a somebody on the streets. Well, that used to be true until after the millennium, when the system got so over crowded they asked for help from the federal government to take over some of their cases. Now in the feds, you have a lot of gun carrying thieves, crack-heads, and dope fiends.

[The "supermax" was made up of an all black staff. It's rare that you see Caucasians that worked there. C.O.'s let us out of our cages from 7am-9:45pm, with an hour lock in for the 3 o'clock count. The food was some bullshit, I could never get used to the taste of it. I went from eating steak and shrimp to eating dog food, while being locked up in a kennel.

[The building was called the "supermax", because of its supermax security level. There was 8 tiers, 4 on the top floor, and 4 on the first floor. [On each tier there are sixteen 10 by 4 cells, each one held two inmates. The tiers were small. The T.V. attached to the wall was so high that you had to lean back in your chair and tilt your neck back to watch it. You were sure to have a neck cramp everyday after watching it. Below the T.V. there were 8 phones. On the side of the phones there is one shower, which was so small that if you dropped your soap or wash cloth you would have to open the door just to bend over to get it. [It was also used for the inmates to urinate in when they were unable to wait until the cells got back open, which opened up every other hour during the day. Me personally, if I dropped any personals on the shower floor, I'd leave it because it was so dirty that you would have to be a piece of shit to save those things. You get one hair cut a week, two visits a week, as well as attorney visits.

[Now you have 32 inmates all watching one TV, sharing 8 phones, as well as one shower on a little tier. There was never a dull moment at the "supermax", it was always something happening. Any day at anytime, somebody could be stabbed, fighting, fussing, but that's nothing compared to the snitching, which in the federal system is better known as the #1 discuss of the human race [A rat would do anything to survive, it's a savage creature.] I was always raised up to honor the #1 code of the streets, you never, ever, I mean ever snitch, not even on your worst enemy and "the game is to be sold and not to be told", sad but true. Many don't honor the code that once kept the secrets of murders, violent acts, and the drug underworld to the street life. Back in the day if you were considered being a "rat", by street law that act was a crime, punishable by death. In this day and time, if you are labeled as being a snitch in some cases, you're honored. If you're a law abiding citizen, not involved in any criminal activity and you tell on somebody, you shouldn't be called a "rat", all you're doing is what your expected to do and cooperate with authorities.

But, if you made the choice to involve yourself in criminal activity, get caught and now try to tell on somebody to get yourself out of trouble, you are a "rat".

The feds were bringing African Americans in by the dozens. 99% of the inmates at the "supermax" all fell victim to the "Boca-Raton" (mouth of the rat).

This goes as far back from the beginning of time. When Adam took the fruit from Eve, God asked him, "Why would you do such a thing after I told you not to bother with the fruit?" Adam told him, "Eve told me to do it." All day long your going to hear "I heard he hot", meaning a snitch.

* The "supermax" had no yard for recreation, instead there was a basketball court and a pull-up bar, which was inside a cage that looked as though it could only fit about 20 inmates in it. Tension was always in the air, so thick that you could cut it with a knife. The female staff, who was sucking and fucking inmates, bought a little joy to the concrete jungle at times. The male staff tried to make it harder for inmates because they wished they had lived the glamorous street life like some of us but without the incarceration outcome. Even the so called rappers, 9 times out of 10, the things they rap about, they didn't do. Those artist are rappin about inmates like me as well as those who shared the "supermax" facility in Baltimore.

Back in the cell, my cousin and I investigated the indictment that was handed down to us by the government for hours. The indictment had several other people who were mentioned but not charged. Little -H's father (big H), Fabo, Yums, Blackron, and a couple others from up their area.

On the "overt Acts", I was the only one that there was no proof, no buys, guns, no drugs or controlled substance in my possession. All of my codee's were charged with these charges, as well as selling to undercover officers. One of the people who got caught in the indictment with the most guns was "low", the same person who got the house arrest instead of me, but I was considered a danger to the community?

* The feds labeled lil-H and his men a gang that terrorized the community of "pioneer city" in Odenton where they lived, as well as sold their product, while doing violent acts. Also, in the indictment, I learned that they spray painted "stop snitchin" on building walls, curbs and mail boxes. They were on some lil boy shit.

Besides the drugs, the main reason why the feds snatched us up was because one of lil-H's men shot a police officer outside of a party in which a co-defendant on our indictment was having. Later, one of them sold the same gun back to an undercover officer, how stupid can you be? In addition, that same night, in the club, they were taking pictures with real guns in their hands showing off for the females. The feds had all the evidence they needed.

The combination of the street knowledge and the person I am, I would've never affiliated myself with these types of people. I later found out that the only person that could've connected me with these niggas was my cousin lil-H. I guess it's true when they say "no good deed goes unpunished".

To me this was a nightmare in which I was waiting to wake-up from. With every second that went by, reality set in deeper and deeper.

While lying on my bunk, I thought back to the days that led me to be in federal custody. My thoughts took me back to Annapolis, "The Capitol of Maryland"

Chapter 3

History

Annapolis—The capitol of Maryland and the home of the United States Naval Academy. It lies along the Severn River on the western shore of the Chesapeake Bay.

The map of the city features two central circles, with narrow streets branching off in all directions. Colonial buildings give Annapolis a historic charm. They include "Paca House", built in 1763 by Governor William Paca; and the "red brick state house", built in 1772. The cities state house is the oldest state capitol still actively used by a legislature. The continental congress met in the state house when Annapolis was the United States capital, from Nov. 26, 1783-June 3, 1784. St. John's college was found as an academy in Annapolis in 1696.

The city is a yachting center, its economy is based heavily on tourism and government activities. The puritans founded Annapolis in 1649. Annapolis was named for Queen Ann of Britain, who gave the city its charter in 1708. It has a Mayor-council government. The city is the seat of Anne Arundel County.

In June 2008, the Baltimore Sun Newspaper released an article on how the crime had increased in Annapolis during the past 10 years. New York's Mayor "Rudy Gulliani", agreed to help the Mayor of Annapolis reduce the murders, drug activity and criminal acts that lie in the city. It's a known fact that if Annapolis had the same population as Baltimore, it would have equal if not by passed their number of murders per year.

C h a p t e r   4

The Past—1979

They say that we're prone to violence, but it was home sweet home for me.

Born at John Hopkins, in Baltimore, I stayed in the hospital for an extra 2 weeks because I was anemic.

I came just a little too early to become an 80's baby. I later learned in life that at the time I was born, it gave me the best of both worlds, in the drug game. "The old and the new money." For that reason I always had an old soul, plus the energy to win in anything I wanted to do in life.

My mother used to say I was a good baby, but 9 times out of 10 that's what all mothers say.

I was short, so I thought that I would always have to prove myself more than others. You might say that I had a small man complex, but I would say that I loved a challenge.

My brother "black", my mother and me, lived where poverty and violence ruled the day, in one of Annapolis' worst projects called "Boston Heights". It was a concrete jungle where your hustle determined your salary. It was a drug infested neighborhood as is the other 9 projects in Annapolis. These communities were no different from any other projects in Maryland. Daylight would've showed any tourist or out of Towner that poverty was prevalent in the "capitol of Maryland". The drug selling seems to never end, all day and all night, the fiends would walk around like the walking dead. This was something like a horror movie, but to me it was also reality.

The crack pipes, needles, baggies, broken glass, and gun shells shared the concrete side walk. Family members would look in disbelief and discuss, as they watched their loved ones rob, steal, and prostitute their bodies for the drug called "crack". The drug dealers took no mercy on anyone who tried to interfere with the cash flow that entered the projects. Many times they would set examples by shooting out of Towner's who came down thinking shit was sweet.

D.C., Baltimore, and New Yorker's (Yankees) heard about the money and tried to come down and claim this goldmine, but they were all unsuccessful. This dispute has been going on before I was born. The out of Towner's who tried to take the fortune learned quickly why the nickname for my city was "Naptown", like many others, who also came down to the capitol and slept on niggas got rocked right into a permanent coma before they even knew what hit'em. Sometimes there were exceptions. There were some that woke up in the hospital knowing they could've lost their life that quick. Just because they thought niggas was soft because they wasn't from their hood.["It ain't where you're from, it's where you're at"] Those who stayed were allowed to only because they fell victim to the drug game in my city, with dreams of going out of town and becoming a king, they couldn't handle the pressure and instead became customers.

Don't under estimate anybody because when you start to sleep on people, some might bring nightmares to reality".

Boston Heights was a death trap, one way in and one way out. We lived down the bottom of the circle, the same building as the laundry mat. I couldn't remember a day that went past without me hearing a gun shot, seeing police, or ambulance lights glowing up the neighborhood like a Saturday in Vegas. My mother would have me and my brother in the house before the sun went down. At first, I wasn't old enough to know why, but my mother knew by knowledge what Boston Heights could have in store for you once them street lights came on. The bus stop, the playground, and the basketball court was at the top of the projects, where the main road was. We rarely got to play up there because my mother couldn't see us and we wouldn't be within eye sight.

Our childhood was normal as any other project child. Birthdays, Christmas, as well as any other holiday's was just like a normal day to us. As we got older we understood that raising two boys was hard enough for our mother, we never faulted her. There wasn't a woman in the world that could take my mother's place.

My mother, a strong woman, the youngest daughter out of eight always kept a job. With the help of the housing authority and food stamps, my mother always kept food on the table and a roof over our heads. The 5 foot 4 inches tall, 150 pound woman never bit her tongue and didn't take shit from anybody. She loved to cook. She used to tell us that being the youngest girl out of eight, she would always help her mother fix food for her brothers and sisters. To enhance her skills of cooking she went to Anne Arundel Community College where she received her culinary degree.

When my mother would go out of town with my Uncles, black and I would stay over our grandparents house out in Bestgate. My grandmother ran the house that sat all the way to the back on the Lincoln Parkway. The woods that surrounded the house kept us and our cousins busy while we visited.

My uncles bought us all bb guns and showed us how to use them. We would all split up as teams and go through the woods and play "war". War was a game our uncles made up by dividing us up into two teams, giving one half a head start in the woods, while the other half would hunt them down, while trying to score points by shooting them with the guns. As we got older we all realized that our uncles were teaching us how to shoot and how to "duck hunt" a nigga down if they ever disrespected the family. Whenever we visited, Ma'Ma made sure that we were taken care of. If any of us ever got out of control she would make us go break a switch off of a tree and ware our ass out.

My grandmother is a strong black woman, who was the back bone of the family. Anyone who helped raise 8 kids, 38 grand kids, 75 great grand kids and 14 great great grandkids had to be strong.

I had three male role models who I look up to, my mother's father was one of them. Standing 5ft 5 inches tall, he didn't take shit from anybody, "a soldier" while growing up, we learned to enjoy watching him kill hogs by shooting them in the head with his rifle. One fourth of his day was spent watching old Westerns. As kids we heard a lot of stories about our grandfather. The one that got my attention the most was when he was younger he shot a police officer because the officer disrespected him at a club called the "DooDrop". The officer wouldn't let him in because he was drunk, my grandfather wasn't going for it. After about 10 minutes of cursing the officer out, he was pushed on the ground by him. Everybody outside the club laughed at him. After getting back up on his feet, my grandfather said "I'll be back!" At that time my grandparents had a house outside of Annapolis near the Severn River Bridge. It took my intoxicated grandfather about 4 hours to walk 8 miles to the house to get his gun and walk back to the club. He crept up on the officer and pushed him from behind. When the police turned around, they said he looked at my grandfather and said "Fuck you want now?" My grandfather pulled his gun out and said "I told you I'd be back", then he shot him. The only thing that saved the officer from getting killed was his belt buckle which didn't allow the bullet to enter his body. My grandfather did 5 years in Jessup prison for that attempted murder, but he made his point.

Besides the 8 kids with my grandmother, he also has 4 others from a previous relationship. 90% of all my family lives in "Naptown", the other 10% lived in the outskirts of Maryland. My grandparents sisters and their families easily equal the "hix" family. Just like my grandparents, their kids, black, myself, and my cousins growing up, if anybody fucked with the family, we all came together like a bunch of hyenas ready to rip shit apart.

My uncles were no strangers to the street life, "Naptown" was familiar with the "Hix Boys". Taking the name and the reputation from their father, they took their share in terrorizing the capitol of Maryland. My Uncles didn't take shit from anybody either, all standing about 5 feet 6 inches tall, they got a lot of money and set a lot of examples in their days. I remember they used to come over to my mother's house when I was young and bag up weed, my mother would always tell me and my brother to stay in our room and don't come out until she said so. One night I snuck out and saw that our kitchen table was full of stinky green stuff that looked like grass. As I got older, I knew that it was weed. My uncles had all types of cars and so many women. I used to witness the women come up to my grandparents house and fight each other over them. All my grandmother could do was shake her head back and fourth and say, "y'all act just like y'all father use too". As my uncles got older, they slowly left the drug game alone and started focusing on being legitimate businessmen. I guess they figured that they did so much dirt in "Naptown" that they had made their mark.

My brother our cousins and me, looked at it as though it was our turn to carry on the name, as well as the reputation that came with it. All of us were considered short, with the exception of a couple who took the opposite parents height.

C h a p t e r   5

The Country

My father was from down the country, that is what Annaplians called Lothian, Maryland. When I was growing up this was the place where I wanted to be 24/7. When I was young I used to cry to go to my grand parents house on the weekends, especially during the summer time.

My father was the oldest out of the 4 kids my grandparents had. My grandmother was a 3rd grade retired school teacher of 27 years, strong black woman. Anytime that I needed anything, if she could help me out, she would. By me being the oldest grandson and looking so much like my father, I think that was the reason she showed me a little more love. Although I looked like her oldest born child all over again, she didn't want me to follow in his foot steps. So as long as I can remember, every time I would visit, she would always teach me the spelling and the meaning of words. I really didn't understand how important school was back then, but now that I'm older I realize how it helped me understand a lot of things in life.

My father told me many stories about him growing up. One that interested me was the one he told me about the first time he got shot by his father at the age of 17 years old. He told me that the reason was because he didn't want to follow my grandfather's rules.

My father and his father are my other two role models, both were soldiers who didn't take shit from anybody.

My grandfather died when I was about 7 years old. I still remember it like it was yesterday. When he used to take me to the store in his old car, that looked like the car on the movie "The God father". I later learned in life that was the one reason I fell in love with antique cars. My Grandfather was a strong black man and had a look on his face that said "I wish you would".

My father inherited that same look and attitude that also got handed down to me. My father, to me, was considered a "gangsta", he used to wear dress clothes and shoes all day like he was in the mob. He had a swagger like no other. He carried a knife with him 24/7 with the exception of the sawed off shot gun, if things got out of control. My mother used to always tell me how she used to fight girls back in the day when her and my father were in a relationship because he wanted to be a player.

My father was also shot two times by the police when he was about 21 years old, because him and some of his comrades robbed a store. Instead of my father giving up, he decided to hold trial on the streets. When I was about 9 years old I asked my father, "why you carry that knife in your pocket?", he said, "in case niggaz act up", I said, "then why you carry that sawed off shot gun with you sometimes?", he said, "because sometimes that's the only thing people understand".

My father and my two uncles, who were known down the country as the "Walders boys", took their share in terrorizing the Lothian, Maryland area when they were growing up. When I was about 10 years old my father said to me, "Booh", when you were first born you were crying hard while me, your mother and everyone around you were smiling." "Live life to the fullest, that way when your at your funeral you're the one smiling while everyone around you is crying . . . you gotta have respect though, if you want respect, you'll have to earn it." The first time he told me that I asked him, "how do you earn respect?", he said, "to earn respect you have to give respect . . . but if a nigga is just a disrespectful person, then fuck' em, because niggas gonna hate you for whatever you do. They get no respect at all, be royal in your own fashion. Act like a King, to be treated like one. Make the best of your today's be the worst of your tomorrows."

For those who don't know, the country is somewhat like the city, the only difference is instead of buildings and concrete, there were dirt roads and trailers that the fiends used to get high in, while the drug dealers made their money.

I learned at a young age that you could make more money off "crack" down in the country then in "Naptown". If you break down an ounce of crack in "Naptown", you could make about $1,200.00, down in the country you could make about $2,000.00.

What separated the drug world down in the country was 2 major streets, "Scott town lane and Sands road". Scott town lane was down shady side and sands road was where my family on my father's side stayed.

Sands road was about a 10 mile long road that had about 3 trailer courts that were drug infested. There was a camp ground on sands road where tourists would come get away from the city life, not knowing that they were in a "danger zone".

On my father's side, most of my family lived on sands road. My grandfather has a sister, who is one of my favorite aunts, and lived on this road with her family. I didn't have a lot of cousins like I had up in Naptown, but there were enough of them. When I would visit, most of the time would be spent over my cousin "C's" house. We were around the same age and used to get into all types of stuff. Stealing from candy stores, taking bicycles, dirt bikes, etc . . . We used to have so much fun. I loved it down there because I had a lot more freedom. Plus, I didn't have to worry about getting hit by a stray bullet as much as if I was up in Naptown. Don't get it twisted though, niggas down the country would bang that iron just as quick as any city slicker.

The "country boys" is what they were called, and just like Naptown they didn't take to kindly to strangers. Come down those dirt roads uninvited if you want, them country boys would blow your back out and burry your body in the woods "quick". The only reason I got a pass was because I was family.

Sands road and Scott Town Lane would always beef with each other. The continuing beef has been going on before I was born. The competition of drug money and the fiends kept the tension so thick between the two crews that shoot outs and drive bys were random.

Back then, instead of going to local cities to party, the "river bend" was the club that everybody went too. It was a hole in the wall and also was a "Death Trap". It was likely that someone was going to get shot, stabbed or just beat the fuck up. Part of it most of the time was because of the two streets beefin. "C" and I used to sneak out his house on weekends and ride our bikes down to the club and watch from across the street. I remember when the Godfather of GO-GO "Chuck Brown" performed down there, it was jammed packed at the club. It never fails though, right after Chuck got off the stage somebody from out of town got stabbed up real bad. When the ambulance got there they pronounced him dead on the scene. That was the last time that the club was opened.

The money and the excitement wasn't the only reason why I loved the country, there was also the females. My cousin "Meka" whom I always looked at as being my sister, used to hook me up with a lot of her girlfriends. She was a leader and with that came an attitude which she carried around with her. Most family members wouldn't get on her bad side because they knew she wouldn't let anything slide easy. Meka caused more family feuds then Richard Dawson. We were always tight since we were practically babies and we would never let anything or anyone come between us.

Chapter   6

Managing Money

West Annapolis elementary is where I went to school for a year. I stayed at my grandparent's house on Bestgate. It was an ok school I guess, even back then I had money on my mind.

Every morning before school, I would go to the store down the street and buy some "now-laters". I still remember it like it was yesterday, when one of my classmates asked could he have a now-later, I said, "you got some money", he said, "how much", I said, "give me a dollar for a pack". He reached in his pocket and handed me a dollar bill with no problem. Now let me remind you that I paid 25 cents for the pack of now-later's and I just sold it for a dollar. I made a quick 75 cents profit. If that ain't a hustler than what is it? That day for me was a big change, from being laughed at for having a free lunch ticket and hand me down clothes to now having something that my classmate's wanted, my self esteem went to the roof.

After that experience, I was bringing candy to school everyday. My clientele went to the roof. For the kids who didn't want to buy packs, I would break them apart and sell individual now-later's for 20 cents a piece. There were six singles in a pack, so if you broke it down, I would make $1.20. I was going to make out one way or another. If a kid wanted to buy more than one pack, I would more then likely give them a deal.

I was bringing about $20.00 a week home, that was a lot of money for a 9 year old coming from where I came from. At the end of every week day, I would take my profits and stash it under the mattress and re-up at the store with the rest of it. I used to be in love with counting my money, all day every day. Niggas in my city called it paper therapy because the money relaxed us. Every time I would go down to the country I would use my stash money to get stuff I wanted. The kids in my school saw how much money I was making and tried to jump on my team. I picked the best two qualified students and gave them a shot at the "American dream". They were doing good for about a week, but then they started slipping. One was eating the candy and the other was trickin with the females. I dismissed both of them because I couldn't have anybody interfering with my cash flow.

I learned how to buy product that kids wanted for a low price and sell it to them for a profit. More importantly, I learned how to manage money at a very young age. About a couple of months later my mother caught me counting my money upstairs over my grandparents house, she said with a serious look on her face, "where did you get that from?", I said, "I was selling candy in school", she said, "I don't want no teachers calling this house because you selling candy in school", I said, "ok". The look on her face was telling me that she wanted to say more but didn't. I know my mother didn't want me to live the life of crime like my father, I could see that the thought just scared her to death. Before she left she said, "I was around your age when I was selling candy in school also". That's when I realized that getting money was in my blood.

Chapter 7

Supermax-Present

The "supermax" at night time was the loneliest times in the feds. Night time gave you time to think about what you did in the past and what you think your facing in the future.

I got out of bed about 12:30am to take a piss in the stainless steel toilet, right after I started, I felt something run across my feet. When I looked down I saw this big rat run out underneath the door, scared the shit out of me so much I almost pissed on myself.

The mice and rats were so brave that they'd come out in the day time and feed off the remainders that the inmates would leave around. Some would set traps for the diseased creatures, once they were caught, the inmates would drop them in the toilet and watch them swim for their life until they'd drown. After getting back on my bunk, lil-h looked down and said, "you going to breakfast yo", I said, "yeah", he said, "if I ain't woke, get me up my nigga", I said, "alright". Trying to get comfortable on the concrete bed with the paper thin mattress was always a challenge. You heard all types of noises at night time over the "max" [Niggas would be screaming, hollering, and banging on the cell doors trying to stop the abuse the small cells held inside] After my body and the cold concrete bed came to an agreement, I went out like a light.

C h a p t e r   8

Annapolis Woods

M y mother moved us out of "Boston Heights" because it was getting too crazy. At the age 13 we were living down in "Annapolis Woods". "Woods" was another one of Naptown's projects that had all the project qualifications. It had two ways you could come in and exit out, that made it easier for the crack heads to drive up, get their product and go out the opposite way. The gun shots rang out all hours of the night and it never discriminated during the daytime. The crack smoking and on going drug sales seemed to never end on Bens Drive. I used to hang out with the "woods boys", which was a bunch of kids who used to go around and do their share of terrorizing Naptown.

Our mothers didn't get abortions, but sort of our fathers did. All of us in reality were raised by the streets. This wasn't going to be me for long though, because I was going to be far from a son who Naptown fathered. We used to go to parties and start fights with neighborhood rivals that lived in Naptown. One week we might be beefing with "Robinwood boys", next week we might be beefing with "Bywater boys". That's how it was growing up in Naptown.

There was never a dull moment that happened in Annapolis Woods. Surprisingly, Woods was where I first had sex, her name was "miny". She had a nice body, brown skin, nice pretty hair, and was a freak at a very young age. I had sex with her down one of my comrades house, I learned how to have sex by watching nasty movies, and from the streets. After lying on top of her about 8-10 pumps, it was all over with. I didn't know if it was good or bad because that was my first time, but just like a kid with his first candy, I was turned out ever since.

One of my comrades, who had high rank in our crew, was "mickeen". He was a soulja, a big youngin and was the oldest out of all of us. Sad but true, later when we got older he got sentenced to life and was sent out to the "cut annex" for a murder in which two of my other so called comrades testified in court against him. That's friends for you huh?

Down Woods is where I got my first real look at the "drug game". I would watch how the fiends beg, prostitute, and get beat down for the crack cocaine. I observed how the dealers would count their money all day out in clear view, like they were working a legitimate business. They wore stylish clothes and drove all the luxury cars. I'm not going to lie, I fell in love with the life style that they were living.

C h a p t e r 9

Admiral Oaks

Boston Heights was getting crazier by the day. The mayor of Annapolis was fed up and decided to close the project down and remodel it. A.P.D. (Annapolis Police Department) couldn't control the people that helped terrorize the community.

After giving all the residents 60 day notices that the project would be closing down, the mayor knew that they wouldn't leave easily. After the 60 days notice was up, the mayor sent the National Guard into the jungle to make sure that everyone who was left vacated the area without any problems. Most residents were relocated to other projects in Naptown while others went to live with family members and loved ones. I remember seeing on the news that they had found a 13 foot snake in one of the apartment rooms. Like I said, "A concrete jungle."

It took about 2 years to remodel the community. With a new look came a new name, "Admiral Oaks", Nick name "Oaks". My aunt's daughter Tonya had gotten a place down there on admiral drive and she offered to let me stay with her. She was always up in Baltimore, so most of the time I had the apartment to myself.

Admiral Oaks was laid back, it didn't have all the qualifications that the old projects had, but there were still shoot-outs every now and then, just to let people know that the reputation of the blood that once soaked the ground was still there. Oaks was where I first had a relationship with an older woman. Her name was "Nickeana", she was from Philly, about 23 years old and I was 14 at the time. She moved to Naptown about a year ago. Nickeana was about 5 feet tall, cute face, sexy body, with the hair style like Hale Berry. She definitely was my first love with a woman.

Yeah she had a nigga, "whipped". If my mother only knew what she was teaching her youngest son in bed, she would've had a fit. Neckeana moved back to Philly later that year. They say that love is painful, and it helps you grow, well she left me heart broken. I got over it though because there were plenty more after that.

In the morning, I used to catch the school bus at the top of Admiral Oaks, to go to Bates Middle School. What ever I was doing the night before, I wouldn't let it stop me from doing good in school. I wasn't planning on being one of those dumb ass niggas out there with no education, I needed that.

It was a lot of girls in the school, but the best part was that a lot of kids were smoking weed. I bought an ounce of weed from this old head nigga out Oaks named, "Mark". He sold it to me for $50.00 and told me that it was some "exotic" stuff, he lied. I had that shit for about a month until I said "fuck it" and practically gave that shit away. The weed didn't even have any smell to it, and on top of that it had a lot of stems also. I realized that if I was going to get into the drug game that cocaine was going to be the product for me to sell.

My cousin started to stay home more because she had gotten a new boyfriend named, "Damien". He was from up Baltimore off Monument Street. We connected with each other with no problem. After a short vote he was adopted into the family. Damien was a soulja from day one. He was behind us 100%, right or wrong. We all had each others back.

C h a p t e r   1 0

Supermax Present 2005

"Fed up!" It was about 5:30am when the C.O. opened the door up so that we could eat breakfast. I got up, tapped my cousins bunk and said, "breakfast yo", we both got up, walked out of our cell, down the stairs and grabbed our tray, and an orange juice. Soon as we stepped back into our cell, the door closed back up just like clock work. I sat on my bunk and studied the so called breakfast meal that the max had made for us. The oatmeal, boiled eggs, and biscuit, which was hard as shit, was probably one of the best meals a lot of these niggas had in a while. I ate the oatmeal and the biscuit because I hadn't eaten since yesterday when I was at the courthouse at 101 Lombard. I gave my cousin the eggs, he seemed to enjoy it just fine. The orange juice was the best part of the meal, but the problem with that was that the staff didn't give you enough. The little carton that the juice came in wasn't enough for a 5 year old to drink. Lil-h said, "yo, Booh", I looked up at the top bunk and said, "whats up yo?" He said "in the indictment they say that I served somebody a half ounce of crack on May 10th?" I tried to beat my head in to see who did I serve, and come to find out it was that nigga "low". That nigga kept calling me that day for the half ounce. I told him that I would holler at him later on. That nigga came knocking at my door a couple of minutes later. I was ready to smack the shit out of him for coming to my house, but I still sold him the half ounce.

I looked up at him and said "Yo"! . . . I told you to leave that nigga alone". He looked at me with a stupid look on his face and said "I know Yo". I told him and his father the same thing about the niggas they was fuckin with," LEAVE THEM ALONE!" They decided not to listen though, even a broken clock is right two time's out of the day.

After eating I laid back down on my bunk and tried to get a couple more hours of sleep before the C.O's opened back up for recreation.

Right before I was about to give my cousin the reason's why we were in federal custody, a nigga outside our cell started screaming real loud. I got to my feet to see what the fuck was going on. Through our cell door I saw another nigga with a big ass "SWORD" (knife) choppin the shit outta that nigga.

The C.O called the code, I guess he saw all that blood and decided not to come up there. By the time the other C.O's got to our block and up the stair's, that nigga was dead. He looked some what like a gutted pig.

The staff wrestled the person with the knife down to the ground where they took the sharp object from him. After about 5 minute's of spraying him with mace, they finally got him off the block. The blood that soaked in the front of our cell door with the combination of mace, smelled like strong hot inside's of a human body. After about an hour of taking picture's the C.O's finally got an orderly to come and clean it up.

Everybody on the block was awake now, hollering up and down their wanting to know what happened. Through all the loud noises, the C.O's informed us that we wouldn't be coming out for recreation until lunch time.

Chapter 11

Eastport

Eastport was off of President street on the 1100 Block. It was a world of its own. Eastportericians was the name given to the boys way before I moved over there. The area was a "Red Zone", meaning that gun shot's, drugs sales, violence seemed to never stop.

Eastport was at the top of the list for the most dangerous place in the Capital of Maryland. It was a place where Drug King's were breaded. Any and everybody from the city would tell you since way back in the late 80's that Eastport was the #1 spot where Hustlers from Naptown would come to buy Weight. It'll be so much Coke being cooked-up over in Eastport at times that you could literally smell it throughout the projects. The super stars in the game played the MAD scientist role on a daily basis.

I remember back when I was young, how I use to hear stories about Eastport and 20-Boys beefin at Annapolis High School or out the mall etc . . .

Eastport was the only neighborhood that had two Projects put together, "Eastport Terrace and Haber House". The only thing that separated the two projects was a side walk and a swimming pool. What's really crazy is that the two hoods use to beef with each other back in the day over territory because of the drug game.

Eastport Terrace looked just like the projects on the movie "Training Day". "The Jungle", is what A.P.D called it. Harbor House looked like a smaller version of one of New York's Borough's.

I was about 14 teen year's old when the Housing Authority transferred my mother's residents over to Eastport. My brother decided to stay out

Bestgate because he had a lot of friend's out there. Not me though, I wanted to see other thing's that I could get my hand's into, mainly money.

*[The very first night we stayed over there a person got slumped right out front our door step. That was the first time I saw a dead body laying on the ground bleeding, taking its last breath. While looking out my window I stared at the newly deceased, and I knew right then and there that shit just got real. I had nightmares for months about that moment.[See, when death comes to one, it comes to us all. It reminds us that any day could be your last day on earth. That was my first time seeing someone actually die in front my face, but it definitely wasn't the last.

Every day when I would come home from school, I would walk down Woodz to go and hang out with my old comrades. I use to notice how some of the same cars and niggas that was down Woodz was over Eastport. One of my comrades informed me that Eastport and Woodz niggas was in alliance with each other. That worked out perfect for me because I hung with the Woodz Boy's and I lived over Eastport, that was gonna be more money for me.

It wasn't a day that I could remember ever not thinking about money, the paper was on my mind 24/7. I never wasted my time like the average teenager sitting in the house playing video games. "Fuck That". I convinced myself that I was born to get money.[When I was younger I always told myself that if I even got into the Drug Game it was gonna be for five reason's; #1 for the money, #2 for the rich's, #3 for the bitches and 4-5 for the snitches

I got cool with three kids over in Eastport, Killa, Riley and Half-Dead. We ran the streets like drunk's run street lights. In time we learned to live the life of crime. We were dirty little kid's with one thing on our mind, "how we was gonna get this money". Without the drug Game, we project kids don't have any way to eat. The late great Malcom X once said "By Any Means Necessary".

My new friend's hooked me-up with all types of females over in Eastport. You know how it is when there's a new face in the neighborhood, all the girl's wanted a piece of the fresh meat. Even a couple of their mother's wanted to feel young again, if they caught my eye, I didn't discriminate. Yeah I was a motherfucker.

The next day we decided to meet-up over my man Half-Dead's apartment over in Harbor House. Soon as I walked into the building I smelled piss and weed smoke in the hallway. We all decided that since we had no startup money that the best thing we should do is sell "Gank" (look alike crack). We melted candle wax, mixed it with baking soda and made it into the form of crack. In addition, we also added Oral Jell in case any of the fiend's wanted to see if the product would numb their tongue. I was fienin to live the good life, but the fiend's were just fienin. We were like Mad scientist. The ounce that we made of the Gank, we split it 4 way's and decided to sell it down Woodz. We couldn't sell it over Eastport because the fiend's knew where we lived and they wouldn't hesitate to go and tell our mother's. Further more, the Eastporterican's who hustled would try and kick our ass for fucking-up the cash flow over there.

We went down Woodz and posted at the bottom of Bens drive so that we could catch all the fiend's before they made it up the top of the projects. By the end of the night, we had about $300, which was gonna be used for start up money. The next day we decided to buy a "Quarter ounce" from a neighborhood super star named "Ike". He was one of the main Drug Dealer's down Woodz, who had been getting money since back in the 80's. We bought the quarter ounce from him, well at least that's what he said it was. We went across the street to a friend's house and dropped it on the scale, it red "5.4 gram's". That nigga worked us, he owed us 1.6 grams. All that hard work that we put into getting that $300, that nigga Ike going to try and work us, "Fuck that! For a couple of minute's we decided to grab a couple of knives out the friend's house and walk back across the street and chop his ass-up. After coming back to reality, we decided not to, because we knew from the word on the street that Ike wasn't no whore, he had a reputation of having an impatient trigger finger. We took the weight back across the street to holler at him about this situation.

I said "Ike . . . Ike! He turned around and said, "what's up young bloods". Killa said "that shit short yo, you owe us 1.6 grams." Ike snatched the crack outta Riley's hand, pulled his scale out of his pocket and dropped the product on top of it. He said "Damn, young bloods ya'll right." He pulled out a sandwich bag filled with big crack rocks, broke a piece off and dropped it on the scale. He said "there ya'll go young bloods. I gave ya'll some extra's." When we looked at the scale it red 8 gram's, you could literally see the dollar sign's in our eyes. Before we left Ike said, "as long as ya'll stay committed and loyal to one another and don't get greedy, ya'll gonna make some money in this game, But also remember that it's a dangerous game to be played. Don't take shit from nobody, if a nigga act like a worm then you put his ass in the dirt. Always remember young bloods, keep your friend's close and your enemies even closer, but only if you know whose who." "Being on this paper trail ain't no telling where it will take you . . . Success needs no explanation, but failure allows no alibis, cause jealousy and envy comes with the territory."

At that time in my life, I didn't know what he was talking about, but as I got older, I realized what he was saying. We bought weight from Ike every time we got finished the package before, he played fair. In the beginning the streets was robbing us though, because we weren't educated enough, but we learned fast. All the money we made in about a month we split 4 ways to where as each of us had enough to start buying our own weight.

[Ike got locked up by the feds at the end of the year, later they gave him a life sentence for the "Rico Law".]The drug game never changes. There is always somebody else in line to take the position of the one before. We started to holler at numerous people out of the projects. I was trying to live the "American dream" from a criminal stand point. You had to be a hustler to know how I felt. I mean to visualize it is like a "coke rush". Playing in the game was an unexplainable high. You had to live it to have felt it. The feeling was better than any and every drug combined.[The first through the fifth was like hitting the lottery to me and the other so called hustlers, who were playing the game. In reality the only numbers that we were guaranteed to get was a jail sentence, that was going to be given to us by a judge or the number of days we had left on the streets before the grim reaper paid us a visit.

We used to give fiends crack so that we could use their cars and joy ride, we called them "rental rocks". That's how I learned how to drive a stick shift. Why not burn somebody else's shit up instead of your own. Everything was going good for me until that one night down Woodz, when I got locked up. Me and about 7 others were sitting on a parked car, when the police rolled up on us. One was "Maralice" who we called the "flunky", and the other was Officer "Bossman". Bossman was a white racist veteran cop who looked just like Jack Nicholson. He was known through out the projects in Naptown for harassing the local drug dealers. People say that the reason was because his daughter died of a crack cocaine overdose. Her black boyfriend, who her father never approved of, supposedly got her hooked on the drug.

When they got out of their vehicles and started to walk towards us, niggas started to walk away. Me, being dumb, decided to sit there. Bossman said, "we got a call saying there was drug activity around this car", I said,

"I don't know what you're talking about". After he searched me and ran my name through the system, everything came back clean. As I was about to walk away the flunky said, "Hold up!" With a smart look on my face, I said, "Hold up for what?" The flunky said, "for this". He pulled out a gun and a sandwich bag filled with cocaine. You know a persons first reaction to this is, "that shit ain't mine". Bossman smiled at me then said, "its yours today". After giving me the joker smile he was famous for, he put the hand cuffs on me and I was driven to the police station.

At the station they tried to question me about the stuff they found. I wasn't a dummy, because I've learned enough from the streets that in a situation like this you need to keep your mouth shut. After about a half hour of sticking to my silence, they knew that I wasn't going to do their job for them. After they finger printed me, and took my picture, they charged me as an adult, then drove me to the commissioner's office. The commissioner was a gorilla looking nigga. He looked at me, looked at the charge papers, shook his head from side to side, then gave me "No Bail". I was then taken to the "Detention Center".

The detention center was an adult jail. The inside looked like a dungeon. The steel side is where they put the high security risk niggas. The smell of piss, shit, rotten fruit, and funk was the aroma in the air. The steel side was located on the top floor of the jail, the dorms were located at the bottom of the center. The dorms were cleaner, stable and were only for the low security inmates. I was put on lock-up because I was only 15 years old. I stayed in the 10 foot by 4 inch cell by myself. Niggaz hollered all day and night talking about nothing, because since there wasn't any T.V. down there they were pressed for conversation. Most of the inmates didn't have an education so reading a book was out of the question.

I remember when I was younger, I couldn't wait to go to jail. To me it was a part of life, when a boy becomes a man. Most grown males that I knew had been to jail. My grandfathers, uncles, and my father all in their life time had been victims to the penal system. To me, my male family tree consists of drug dealers, thugs, and killers, a man becomes a man from all the things he goes through, I just put my feet in the foot prints that were left for me without saying a word. So at a very young age, I've been having visions of prison, but after experiencing that shit, it was nothing that I couldn't get used too.

8 o'clock the next morning the C.O. walked to my cell to inform me that I had a bail review around 11 o'clock, he then popped my cell door

so that I could get my one phone call. I called my mother's house and got no answer, I then tried my grandparent's house and my grandmother answered the phone. She informed me that my mother and aunt were on the way to the court house for my bail hearing. After telling me that she was praying for me and me telling her that I loved her, the phone cut off. I went back to my cell for a couple of hours and laid back before the C.O. came and got me for my bail hearing. I was put in a small room with a state's attorney and someone from the public defenders office. The big screen T.V. showed that the judge could see me as well as I could see him. I could hear my mother in the background crying and talking at the same time. Once the judge found out how old I was and that this was my first offense, he agreed to let me go home with my mother until my court date. I was released from the detention center about 1 o'clock that afternoon. My mother and aunt waited on me in the parking lot. You know I got the 3rd degree treatment from her. She yelled, "You're just like your father!" I tried to explain that the stuff wasn't mine, but she wasn't trying to hear it.

Back over at Eastport, I was greeted by my comrades. I explained to them that one of those niggas put that shit under that car and didn't tell anybody that it was there. They told me that they've been asking around to find out who did it, but was unable to get a straight answer.

I got turned on to a good lawyer, Peter O'Neel. In mine and many others opinion, he is the best lawyer in Anne Arundel County. O'Neel was called, "superman" through out the projects in Naptown because he would come in the court room, beat your charges, then fly out of there on his way up to the Glen Burnie court house to beat more charges for somebody else. If the charges were impossible to beat, he would definitely get you the best plea possible. The hustlers in Naptown and through out Anne Arundel County say that O'Neel knew "Black Magic". The flip side to this was that he comes with a high fee.

I made an appointment and went to see O'Neel. After looking over my charge papers, he told me that he's going to charge me $3,500.00 for the case because the first thing he had to do was get my adult charges waived back down to juvenile charges. The $3,500.00 put a dent in my pocket, it knocked me off my feet, but I crawled right back. By the knowledge of the streets, I knew that living the American dream feels good, but more important was lawyer fees.

My point from then on was that I was going to stay focused and get this money. Now I was officially in the "game". When I went back to

Annapolis High School the next day it felt like everybody knew I had gotten locked up. I saw my man "killa" and he informed me that my arrest was all in the newspaper. It felt like all eyes was on me. Before I knew it, I was called down to the office by the principal, where he informed me that I would be expelled until the B.O.E. (Board of Education) saw the out come of my court case.

All I could think about was breaking my mother's heart when she found out that I got kicked out of school. When I got home from school my mother greeted me with a punch to the chest, that let me know that the principal had already got in touch with her. I had never seen her that upset before. All she kept saying was, "your ass going to jail" over and over. Shortly after, she went upstairs and just cried and cried. I felt bad, but I think that was the reason that motivated me to get more money and stay focused. The way I saw it was that I could make a lot of money, get out of the drug game, and use the money to open up a legitimate business. If I became successful, I knew my mother would have been proud of me. All day and all night, I was outside over Eastport, "hustling". I decided not to go back down Woodz to hustle because the police down there knew who I was. I was on a "paper chase" for real.

Chapter 12

Allens Apartments

After a couple of months had passed, my mother left me the apartment over in Eastport and went to stay with her boyfriend out in Allen's apartments. The apartments were another one of Naptowns projects, the only difference was that there were Mexicans instead of niggas, we called them, "SA's". The "SA's ran another neighborhood in Naptown called, "Admirals Furget", they also took their share in terrorizing the Capital of Maryland.

Allen's apartments had all the qualifications as any other projects. The poverty also spread through out this community. The SA's were far from being dumb, they would put their money together every week from working, after paying the bills, buying food, the rest of the money went to buying drugs and tricking with the "colored women". They could barely speak English, so they would come to you and hold up two fingers, letting you know that they wanted to buy twenty pieces of crack. The only real English that I ever heard them speak was, "girl", meaning that they wanted a trick for the night. The SA's would usually beef among themselves. Every night while getting drunk they would start acting crazy with each other, it never failed. Every now and then you might hear about a Mexican and a black person getting into it, but it was rare. The SA's had the Allen apartments looking like little Mexico, had it smelling like "tacos and shit". My mother would come over Eastport everyday after work to cook for me and make sure that the apartment was clean before she would leave for the night.

C h a p t e r 1 3

Blood Sweat and Tears

When I say I grinded, I mean, I "grinded", like a bad pair of break pads. I was bread to get it in, "no spoon". I went to my father's house down in the country and got hooked up with my cousin, "C". My family members knew I got locked up because they read the newspaper and word traveled fast. My father's mother was heart broken when she heard the news. The same route I was taking was the same route her oldest son had taken when he was about my age many years ago. My grandmother, aunt, and the rest of the family continued to show me love as any other family would. All they could tell me is to stay out of trouble, little did they know that I was too far gone in the drug game to quit now.

[My cousin C had the drug game on "lock" down in the country. To my surprise he had his own drug stop that brought in close to $10,000 a night. He had our little cousins, "Hug" and Carlos manage the spot when he was out of town. They were both younger and shorter then me with the heart that was bigger than two giants, with no patience, they ran a bunch of little souljas who called themselves, "the sands road boys". They had guns that you had to hold with two hands, and they weren't faking either. C and the rest of my family, that were in the drug game, welcomed me with open arms.

Through the week I was over Eastport getting money and through the weekend I was down in the country. I was on a rampage because all I could think about was that I was going to jail when my court date came.

A month later I was over Eastport serving a fiend when I got a call from my lawyer, Peter O'Neel. He informed me that he had got my charges waived back down to juvenile charges and that my court date was scheduled for September 12th. I had about two months to continue to get this money before I could possibly be hauled off to jail. I grinded from Eastport down to the country so much that I used to get headaches all the time. Counting the money, serving the fiends and worried about the police, didn't help the situation either.

The officers down in the country were "county cops". Sometimes they would use unmarked cars instead of regular county cars to creep up on us. They always tried to role up on us, but by the time they got down the dirt road, we would already be running through the woods. We knew the woods like the back of our hands and they didn't. Now the police over Eastport were different. The Eastportericans usually hung out in front of the Rec Center to sell their drugs, in that spot you had a clear view in case APD was coming. If we saw a bubble police car, we would holler out "Bubble car", that meant that there were rookies in the car who we weren't really worried about. Now, if somebody yelled out, "box car", then that meant trouble. Box cars were usually driven by somebody from S.D.U. (Special Drug Unit) that the city put together to stop drug activity and lock up drug dealers.

C h a p t e r   1 4

Juvenile Criminal System

I went to court on Thursday, the juvenile criminal system was downstairs in the circuit court building, on Church Circle, in Annapolis. When my mother and I arrived at the court house, we noticed that my lawyer was having a conversation with the prosecutor. After a short period of time he noticed us and made his way in our direction. After greeting each other, O'Neel told us that the prosecutor was asking for jail time. [The look on my mothers face would've given you the impression that she was the one going to jail. O'Neel continued to tell us that if I take the plea that the prosecutor was offering; the gun charge would be dropped and I would do a couple of months in a juvenile detention center for the cocaine charge. Now, if I decided not to take the plea and go to trial and be found guilty, I would be spending the next couple of years in a juvenile facility.]My mother asked my lawyer what did he think was best, due to his experience of the law. O'Neel explained that due to the amount of drugs, the gun, and that I wasn't a resident of the Woodz neighborhood, which is a drug infested area, it's best that I take the plea. I took the plea and got two months at "Shelton Ham Juvenile Facility". They gave my mother full responsibility of turning me into Shelton Ham the next day by 6:00pm. All my mother did for the rest of the day was cry.

When I got back over to Eastport, I saw my comrades sitting on the sidewalk, I informed them that I had gotten a couple of months at juvy starting tomorrow. I told them don't stop getting money because I'm gone, because I was going to need them when I got back home. They all gave me a pound and assured me that they had my back.

I knew that I was going to be alright in Shelton Ham, I spent the
night at the detention center so no juvenile facility could be worse then
that. I didn't get any sleep that night. I started counting my stash money
over and over because I wasn't used to having a lot. I must have gotten
tired of looking at the dead presidents because I finally dozed off. I was
awakened by my brother black about 11:00am. Black was about 5 inches
taller then me and looked like the singer Tyrese. Even though we had the
same mother and different fathers we always had each others back 100%,
right or wrong. He tampered with the drug game a little every now and
then. Black said, "go do those couple of months and come back". If me or
any of my family got to beefin with anybody he was the first one to ride.
He knew he couldn't ride with me this time, I had to take this trip on my
own. Before leaving he looked at me and said, "yo, you in the drug game
now". Black gave me a brotherly hug and then left. He was a soulja and
he knew I was a soulja also. I could still see the hurt in his face knowing
that his little brother was caught up in the street life.

I opened my door to get some fresh air and saw that the same shit
was going on that went on every morning just like clock work. Niggas
were outside shooting dice while the fiends walked around looking like
zombies. After putting my clothes on I walked down Sankies to get a
sandwich and orange juice. When I got back over to Eastport Terrace, I
went over to the dice game. They were betting big money, a $100.00 was
the minimum. My man "Vince", just rolled a 7 on the first roll and won a
thousand dollars, then immediately said, "bet that thousand". I remember
thinking that was the kind of talk only reserved for "bosses".

Vince was big like Biggie Smalls and he looked some what like him
too. This nigga was getting money, I mean "real money". I used to watch
him sit on the side walk for hours shooting dice. Vince wasn't the king
over in [Eastport, he was considered a "Don-Dita", which means "God"
in Jamaica.]The fiends catered to him all day hoping that he would need
one of them to run to the store because they knew that he was going to
reward them dearly. Vince always looked out for hustlers over in Eastport
when they came home from jail or if they needed some help at the time.
Vince always said,["never look down on one of your comrades unless
you trying to help them up"]. He was one of the biggest drug dealers that
came out of the Capital of Maryland. His right hand man was "Bell", he
was a short stocky, light skin nigga. Bell too was getting a lot of money,
which niggas respected. When you see one, you always saw the other.
Neither one of them would hesitate to get you killed if you crossed

them, There was also a few more niggas at the dice game. These superstars were cold blooded East Puerto Ricans. While I was growing up over in Eastport, I watched these hustlers moves and studied their mistakes. They were getting a lot of money and I wanted it just like they were getting it, because "being broke and dirty gives a nigga the chills". All of them had cake and were living the American dream from the criminal stand point.

I had no where near the money or cocaine they had, so in order for me to get money over in Eastport, I had to be smart. These hustlers didn't serve fiends for nothing under $10.00, so I used that to my advantage. I would serve the fiends for their couple of dollars to get my clientele up, where as though they would be so thankful that when they came back with "big money", they would spend it with me.

Out of these East Puerto Ricans, the main one that took me under his wing was "Skip". Skip was a soulja, good dude. He liked me because he saw that I was a little kid trying to come up in the game. He always said that I reminded him of himself when he was around my age. Skip gave me knowledge of all the tricks and trades that came with the drug game. I always considered myself as a leader, I never followed orders, but I always had my mind open for knowledge. I became Skip's number one man, and he was my number one connect. Skip had me flippin 62's like the drug game was going out of style. He looked up from the dice game and said, "what's up shorty?" I said, "ain't nothing", Skip said, "let me holler at you". We walked around the corner, he said, "how you holding up?" I said, "I got 60 days up boys village for that shit underneath of that car down Woodz", he said, "I'm still trying to find out who put that shit under that car without letting niggas know", I said, "soon as you find out, let me know so that I can bless'em. I know that two wrongs don't make a right, but three lefts do". Skip said, "yo, you need to stop fuckin with them, live for the moment ass niggas you be around, they don't think about the future. All they gonna do is cause trouble for you anyway. All them niggas want to do is beef with everybody, fake like they getting money. You can't be no hustler while beefin with niggas. Shorty if you got beef with everybody, then who you gonna sell your product too?"

That shit did make sense though, because I learned that broke niggas don't want no money, they just want to kill you. Skip said, "While you doing that 60 days, think about what direction you want to take in life. If you came to the decision that you wanted to continue to play the game, then you have to start dismissing yourself from being around dumb niggas and doing dumb shit. The only thing that's worse than wasted time is time wasted."

That's why I liked Skip, he always was giving me knowledge. Everything he ever told me out his mouth was all fact and reality. Skip was more like a father figure to me, who wanted to see his only son succeed.

C h a p t e r 1 5

Shelton Ham Juvenile Facility

My mother and aunt got me at the juvenile facility, that was known as "boys village", about 5:45pm. Soon as we saw the jail my mother started crying, I tried to assure her that I was going to be ok, but you know a mother always going to worry about their child in a place like this.

When my mother and I got into the jail gate, we were buzzed in. The lieutenant met us at the door. He said, "what's your name?' I said "Rome Walders", he said "we been waiting for you". The lieutenant informed my mother that I wouldn't be able to call until Sunday because that's the day the facility allowed phone calls by inmates. My mother gave me a hug that seemed like an hour, while telling me that she loved me over and over again. After finally letting go, she told me to call on Sunday.

The Lieutenant called one of his staff members over and told him to get me a uniform and a new man package. After the C.O. made me strip butt naked, he gave me a uniform and told me to get dressed. After I got dressed, I was put into a bull pin with about six juveniles, who also had to turn themselves in and had to go through the same procedure.

"Where you from yo?" One of the little niggas asked. I said, "Naptown." He said, "where that at yo?" The little nigga sitting beside him with the missing teeth in his mouth said, "that's the capital of Maryland dumb ass."

The other juveniles in the bull pin started to laugh at him. I guess some of them little niggas was happy to be there. Me personally, I'd rather be home.

The C.O. passed out the bag lunches which consisted of a bologna sandwich, potato chips and two cookies. The bologna-cheese sandwich smelled sour so I traded it for the cookies.

After eating, the C.O. put all of us on a van and informed us that we would all be going to "Unit 6". Unit 6 was like a ½ mile from where we were.

Boys Village was "Big Ass Shit", you would have never thought it was that size, if you hadn't seen it before. The female juveniles were kept on the other side, you could only see them outside during recreation, only if your eyes could see that far.

One by one we got off the van and entered the unit 6 building. The first thing I noticed was that it smelled like an old person's house.

*[The counselor who looked like "Bill Cosby", met us at the door and informed us that we would all be sleeping in the gym until a cell became available for us.]

Unit 6's capacity was 75 juveniles, all together there were 125 juvy's in the unit. The counselor took us down the hallway to a room stacked with bed mattresses and told us to grab one. [After getting our pissy mattress, the counselor showed us where the bathroom was and advised us to stand on the toilet seat when taking a shit because it's been complaints that kids were catching crabs from it.

The gym was packed, it looked like a shelter for the homeless instead of being part of a recreation area. Inmates stared at us like we were aliens.

The counselor told us to pick a spot on the gym floor and get used to it because we were more than likely going to be sleeping there for a while. After finally finding a spot, I laid on my mattress, stared up at the ceiling and listened to the juveniles talking about what they did to get into "Shelton Ham". The lengthy time seem to not bother many of them.

[The only story that interested me was when the one little nigga who was sleeping beside me, who had a face only a mother could love, told the one across from me how he used to sell heroine off Greenmount Ave, in Baltimore City. His name was "Rock". He bragged about how he had a hundred grams of "raw dope" that was taking a 10. He cut it with mannitol, caffeine and quinine where as though he turned a hundred grams into about a half a brick of scramble. He continued to brag about how broke he was in the beginning of the summer, and for start up money he robbed a drug dealer around his way for close to $10.000.00. He proceeded on saying how he went to his uncles to buy the dope, and that by the time the summer was over, he had about $100,000.00 in his stash. He preached about how he spent a lot of money by taking bitches shopping, smoking weed and gambling. The little nigga across from me asked him how much he had stashed. Rock explained that the D.E.A. (Drug Enforcement Agency) kicked in his door in and used $50,000.00 for evidence and kept the rest of the money for themselves.

I remember thinking, "damn, this little ugly nigga might be telling the truth.", but skip always taught me to "believe half of what you see, and none of what you hear, because talk was cheap and everybody could afford it."

I thought long and hard about what Rock was talking about. Down in Naptown, you never heard of anybody selling dope but you knew that dope fiends was down there. All the dope fiends that I knew drove up to Baltimore everyday and brought dope valves then came back to Naptown to get high. Most of the time the monkey would be on their back so much that they'll snort or shoot the product up before they made it back.

It was always said that "Cocaine will get you rich, but dope will get you wealthy". I didn't get high off anything, except life. So I figured that if I got a serious dope connect, I could become a millionaire in no time.

The same thing went on everyday in Shelton Ham, Inmates fighting and stabbing each other like it was no tomorrow.

I slept in the gym for about 3 weeks, during that time. I made it my business to become cool with Rock. I wanted to live in the American Dream and it was a good possibility that he was going to make it happen for me. We got so cool that we both requested to the counselor that we be put into a cell together, the counselor approved it.

The cell we moved into was filthy, the toilet was stained with shit and the floor smelled of old piss. After a couple of hours of us cleaning the cell, Rock and I talked all that night about the fun each of us had back in our hood. Me being from Naptown and him being from B-More, besides the valves they used to distribute their product, we realized that both of our hoods were the same.

The days dragged on and on. They kept us in the cell on lock-down the whole time, because every time the C.O's would let inmates out for recreation, somebody would fight or get stabbed-up.

I stayed in the juvenile facility for 50 days. I was let out early because of good time. I left up out there with the knowledge and the jewels of getting more money.

C h a p t e r   1 6

The Only People That Seem Perfect at What They Do are Gods and Dead People

The first thing I did when I got home was count my money, and after that I went to look for Skip so that I could buy some weight. I had to make-up for the money that I've missed, while I was gone. I ran into him over Harber house by the pool. After he gave me a fatherly hug he said, "what's up shorty?" I said, "ain't nothing, chillin'", Skip said, "you alright?" I said, "you know me . . . I'm a soulja." He said, "I know you a soulja because if I thought other wise I would have never started showing you love."

Skip informed me that my comrade, Killa got sent up to Hickory Juvenile Facility for stealing a car, and Riley got sent up to Waxters for not reporting to his P.O (probation officer) and half-dead got sent up to the mountains for 18 months.

I said, "damn, my whole little squad is locked up, they were supposed to hold shit down for me while I was gone." Skip said, "I told you that them niggas wasn't going to amount to nothing but trouble, and you don't need that in your life. That little vacation time in boys village, did you think about what direction you wanted to take?"

I said, "yeah, I wanted to continue to play the game." He paused and looked at me with a serious look on his face and said, "some people say that the only thing that's promised is jail bars and grave yards and you got a better chance at hitting the lottery at 999 to 1 than to be successful in the drug game, understand?" With a serious look on my face, I said, "yeah." He said, "The drug game is 24/7 . . . 365 days a year with no days off and with one mistake, nothing would make a difference. The game is only what you make it to be. The only people that seem perfect at what they do are gods and dead people. That mistake that got you sent to boys village was a good mistake because you learned from it. As long as you learn from it, mistakes build character and character can take you places that money can't. Most people play because they try to cheat life because they can't cheat death. So many niggas get so focused on growing in the game they forget why they are in it.

Shorty, it makes no difference what your intentions are or how much money you make, because if you don't have a vision or goal in mind, its just going to be a matter of time before the streets swallow you up. Then the game will start "extorting" you, before you know it, all would've been done for nothing . . . understand?" I said, "I understand." Skip said, "So what's your goal or vision in life?" I said, "huh?" With an attitude, he said, "what do you want out this shit? Because when you piss your pants your only gonna stay warm for about so long. After things come to an end, if [you fail to plan you planning to fail.] I'm going to give you a couple days to bring me an answer . . . and if it's not the answer that I'm looking for then, I'm not selling you nothing no more. I'm always gonna love you, but I'm not gonna be the reason why you fall victim to these streets."

After giving me a fatherly hug, he told me he would see me in a couple of days. Those couple of days dragged on and on. I thought long and hard for the answer that I was going to give him."

I got up early that morning and went outside to look for Skip, I knew he was out there because he was a firm believer that the early bird gets the first worm. I finally saw him talking to some fiends in the park over Harbor house.

"What's up Skip?" After showing me love as usual, he said, "you got something for me?" I said, "yeah" he said, "let me hear it" I said, "my goal is to reach $100.000.00 so I can build a legitimate business from the ground up. After I reach that goal I'll be satisfied . . . that's my vision." With a serious look, Skip said, "I'm a hold you to that, because everybody can hustle but can't everybody be a hustler. Growth is the only evidence of life. Shorty, if you want to grow in this game you got to disassociate yourself with dumb niggas doing dumb shit." I said, "I know"

Skip said, "plan all the way to the end, because the ending is everything, you got to have a plan A and a plan B, your plan A is your dream, but plan B is your reality. Take into account all the possible consequences, obstacles, and twist of fortune that might change your hard work and give your glory to others, because enough money will solve your problems, but to much of it could kill you. First you get the money, then you get the power, then you get the respect. It's best to be loved and feared in this game, but never let one conflict the other because too much love could make you lose focus and too much fear could make you more enemies than your eyes will allow you to see. One thing is for sure, you got to have heart, so when a nigga act a foul, you give his ass two shots and I ain't talking about basketball either. With a serious look on my face, I said, "I understand." He paused for a second then said, "Skies the limit Shorty. So reach for the stars that way if you fall you'll land on a cloud.

Chapter 17

The Cook-Up

Annie-May was one of our neighborhood crack heads who let us use her apartment to cut, cook and bag our product.

She was 5 foot tall and looked like that tails from the crypt dude. All she did was stay in the apartment and got high all day. Her house smelled like dog shit and crack smoke. She always kept her shades down on the windows, so that the sun light wouldn't shine in. She lived like a vampire who had barricaded herself in her casket, scared to show her ugly face in the day light.

She always bragged about how she was going downtown at the Harbor selling pussy to the rich white folk. Annie-May welcomed us in and proceeded to get all the cooking supplies for Skip. With the cryptic voice, she said, "the water was boiling on the stove and there's a fresh box of baking soda, napkins, and a spoon on the counter . . . and don't forget to leave mine on the table." Skip looked at me and said, "come on Shorty, I'm about to show you why they should call me chef E.P.T. (Eastport Terrace)."

In the kitchen, Skip reached in his pocket and pulled out a digital scale and sat it on the table. He then reached in his dip and pulled out a large zip-lock bag filled with pure cocaine.

※ Skip said, "pay attention Shorty, because from now on, your gonna be cooking your own product." Skip dropped the cocaine powder on the scale and it red 125 grams, then he poured it into the pyrex jar that was sitting on the table. He then weighed out the 125 grams of baking soda and poured that into the same pyrex jar. With a regular tea spoon he dipped it into the boiling hot water that was on the stove about 5 times, poured it into the jar. While Skip stirred the mixture, he said, "all the crack that you buy from anybody always got cut on it, so instead of buying crack with cut on it, you gonna be cutting your own product up from now on, plus you gonna make more money."

I said, "that makes sense." After the mixture in the pyrex was pasty like, Skip sat the jar inside the pot with the boiling hot water. Skip said, "watch real close Shorty and make sure that the boiling water never goes below the product because if it does it'll cook the bottom of the cocaine faster than the rest, add water if you need too."

While Skip continued to teach me, he also continued to dip the tea spoon in the boiling hot water and poured it on top of the product.

After about ten minutes, Skip took a cloth, grabbed the pyrex handle and raised it out the boiling hot pot. While swirling the hot pyrex around, Skip looked at me and said, "see Shorty . . . that's how you cook."

The expression on my face was as if I had just seen the greatest magic trick done right before my eyes.

Skip opened the refrigerator door up and said, "Damn", I said, "what's wrong?" He said, "that bitch Annie-May ain't got any fuckin ice cubes.

I said, "what's the ice for?" He said, "After the work is ready to come out of the pyrex, you have to cool it off so that it can get hard."

Skip then turned the cold water on in the sink and gently used his hand to splash it on top of the product. After being satisfied with the work, he then took the product out of the jar and put it on top of the napkins so that it could dry out.

The crack looked like a big ass rice cake. After a couple of minutes, Skip took the product and dropped it on the scale. He then looked at me and with a smile said, "come read the scale." I walked behind the counter and witnessed that the scale read 155 grams.

I said, "damn, you gained an extra 30 grams." Skip looked at me and said, "see Shorty, when you cook your own product up you gain more every time, if you know what you're doing." I said, "that's more money for me," Skip said, "all powder cocaine ain't the same . . . fish gail powder cooks faster than bage powder, but bage powder due to the oil base, gains more weight if you cook it right."

I said, "how do you know what kind of powder you got?" Skip said, "whenever you get your powder see if there is any crystals sparkling in it, if so, then you got fish gail . . . if you don't see any then it's bage, and you either got bage cocaine, or your product got a lot of cut on it. Remember garbage is always going to be sold out here on the streets, that's why it's called the game, because if every hustler had good coke without the garbage then we all would have the top dollars. It won't be called the game anymore it'll be called the way. Just the same way you ride a bike." I said, "why is it called fish gail?" He said, "because the powder is similar to the gills on the fish when the sun hit it." I said "Oh alright"

Skip said, "don't ever cook cocaine in the microwave because it takes the spunk out of the product. Always keep the product in coffee because it stops the police dogs from trying to sniff it out." I said, "I'm going to remember." I brought the 155 grams from Skip for a nice price. He told me that he gave it to me for that price because he knew that I was trying to get back from that time that I was gone to "boys village". I appreciated it.

Before leaving, Annie-May yelled out, "don't forget to leave mine on the table!" Skip looked at me and said, "go ahead Shorty, that's part of being in the game. You can't inhale without exhaling." I blessed her by leaving a gram on the table, it was a "ritual."

From that day on, my whip (cook) game was at a professional level.

Chapter 18

Higher Learning

Annapolis High was nothing but a fashion show. The school brought the white and the poor black kids together for education. My mother didn't hesitate to go to the board of education so that I could get back into school. After months and meeting with the principal, I was back at Annapolis High before I knew it. No matter how long I was outside hustling, I always got up the next morning and went to school. I figured I owed my mother that much for all the trouble I had been putting her through.

I got good grades and stayed focused while I was at school. I liked going to school, besides the females, shooting dice in the bathrooms, there was also money to be made in school.

The rich white parents who sent their kids to school for education never knew that their loved ones were really getting a "higher" learning than usual. I sold powder cocaine to the rich kids for $100.00 a gram, every week I was bringing home about $2,500.00 from my so called classmates. The other kids saw the money I was making, the stylish clothes I was wearing and wanted to get it like I was getting it. I gave two kids a shot at the "American dream" to see where their minds were. Everything was going good for about a week, then both of them niggas started slipping. One was coming up short with the money and the other was using the product to trick with the females. I had to dismiss the both of them, it was like "déjà vu" all over again from when I was back in elementary school.

My reputation for getting money got around fast and you know what comes with money, "Girls." I used to catch a cab to my house over Eastport with different females almost every other school day at lunch time. After I gave them the business I would always make sure I was back at school before my last class started. If she was average, the bathroom in school would do just fine.

I remember when career day came to our school. The guy from the military asked me would I like to join the Army? I said, "yeah right" then walked out of his face. Both of my grandmothers always said, "That's the white man's war", furthermore what I look like going to another country and fighting some people who don't even care about their own lives. This country was going to need more then just a few good men to win that war. I was earning my "purple heart" right here in the United Snakes of America, home of the slaves and land of the beast.

The basketball and football games were like a club night on the weekends in Naptown. Everybody and their mother came out to the games. You would have thought it was a car show the way the drug dealers had their whips out in the parking lot.

After the games were over, the McDonald's across from the Annapolis Mall was like the after party. It would be so packed outside the restaurant that you had to park at the mall or the high's parking lot.

Every time Annapolis played Mead High and Old Mill High there was always an altercation. For that matter, there was always extra security when the teams played each other. For an outsider, I guess you might say that it was war, and about who owned Anne Arundel County. I used to envision about coming together with "free-town, Pioneer City and Mead Village" to start getting money. I knew it was going to be hard, but I was determined to make this happen.

C h a p t e r 1 9

The Route

Without Risk There Is No Reward

Officer Bossman got word from one of his snitches on how I was coming up in the game fast. I wasn't worried about it though because even blind eyes like Stevie Wonder could see that I was getting money.

During the last couple of years he tried to lock me up for selling drugs, driving without a license and loitering, My lawyer "O'Neel" would always get the charges dismissed.

I remember when me and "white boy Mike" had words with each other because I told him to stop selling "gank" over at Eastport. He was a dope fiend trying to support his habit by getting over on other fiends. The next day they found his body in his car over Harbor house with a bullet in his head. Bossman got word from one of his informants that I killed him. 10:00am the next morning, I was walking down to Sanky's to get my usual, I saw a box car turn off president street on to Sanky's street. I knew it was Bossman and his Flunky.

I said, "Ah Shit!" Bossman said, "put your hands behind your back." I said, "for what," he said, "you going to jail for murder-one," I ain't kill nobody," I replied. He said, "Yeah right."

After Bossman put the handcuffs on me, the flunky patted me down and then threw me into the back of the police car. I wasn't really worried about what Bossman said, but I was worried about that 8-ball I had in my dip.

At the top of President Street instead of him making a right to go towards the police station, he made a left.

I said, "where y'all taking me!" Bossman said, "your ass going down Bay Ridge to Homicide."

While riding pass Annapolis Woodz, I made a decision to swallow the crack that was in my dip instead of giving these racist motherfuckas the satisfaction of finding it on me. The salty taste of the crack almost made me vomit, the numbness of my mouth and throat had me thinking that I probably shouldn't have swallowed that shit.

✳ [The homicide building was past the Giants, beside a graveyard.]

Bossman got out of the car and walked into the building for a couple of minutes. The flunky stared at me in the back seat for a couple of seconds, then said, "we missed you."

I said, "I told your mother the same thing last night." Then I started to laugh out loud. He said, "you'll see smart ass."

Bossman came back to the car, opened the door then said, "get out asshole"

When I got into the small dark grey building, there was a desk, chair, and two single man cells. Bossman uncuffed me then said, "take everything off drop and squat."

After stripping naked and squatting, the flunky searched my pockets to see what he could find. Bossman said, "1300.00!" Then he smiled at me with his famous joker smile. The flunky looked at me and said, "my kids are gonna eat good this week."

Bossman then threw my clothes at me and said, "get dressed." After putting my clothes back on I said, "I aint got nothing to say to ya'll, and I want to call my lawyer." Bossman looked at the flunky and said, "throw his ass in the cell"

The cell had one bed, one toilet, and a smell that I couldn't explain. I was left in the cell for about 4 hours. Inside the cell I tried to throw up the crack that now had me feeling like I was about to pass out. I forced myself to drink the foulest water from the nasty sink so that I wouldn't get dehydrated. I could literally feel myself about to faint. Everything around me started to spin out of control. Right when I was about to call Bossman to tell him take me to the hospital, the flunky came jingling the keys towards the cell. He took me out the cell, put the cuffs on me and walked me outside. When we got outside, Bossman was in the drivers seat just watching me while the flunky put me into the back seat of the car. With a disappointed look on his face he said, "while we had your ass down homicide, we got a search warrant for your mother's house over at Eastport Terrace and we found a triple beam scale in your closet." I thought to myself, I need to go to the hospital." Bossman then informed me that my mother would be getting charged also because her name is on the lease. To myself I said, "Damn, my mother gonna be mad as shit."

When I got to the police station, Bossman let me make a phone call. I called, "Pack-O-Bails Bond" to let him know that I was going to need him to bail me out in about an hour.

After the usual routine at the police station, they took me to the Commissioners office. The whole ride there Bossman talked mad shit to me, while the flunky just laughed and agreed with everything he said. Before I was guided into the Commissioner's office, Bossman told me that he was gonna get me for murder sooner or later and that I was going to be watched 24/7. I didn't give a fuck what he was saying because at that point I could feel myself passing out.

Either I was high from the crack I swallowed or the Commissioner really did look like a monkey with glasses on. He looked at my charge papers, then looked at me and said, "you don't look so well."

I said, "I think I caught something in that nasty ass cell that A.P.D's finest had me in."

After punching on the computer for a couple minutes, which seemed like hours because the crack had me tripping. The Commissioner looked at me and said, "I am going to let you go on your own recognizance."

I was surprised about that because the type of person that I was, usually always got to pay one way or another.

The flunky uncuffed me, while Bossman just stared at me with an evil look on his face. I smirked at him then, asked, "can I get my money back ya'll took?"

Bossman said, the police dog detected that there was drug residue on it so your money is being confiscated by the city of Annapolis. That was bullshit because if that was the case half of the money in the world got residue on it.

Bossman said, "in order to get your money back you need to get a lawyer to file a motion.", which was also bullshit because first you have to show proof of where the money came from, then your lawyer is going to want half of it as a fee for representing you. I said, "fuck that money!"

While I walked out of the Commissioners office, Bossman and the flunky followed behind me. I turned around and said, "what now?'

Bossman reached in his pocket pulled out a five dollar bill and threw it at me. I said, "fuck I'm going to do with this?" He said, "use it to get your ass back to the projects." I said, "yeah right"

While I walked out to the main road, I was glad that he threw me that money because now I had money for cab fair to the hospital.

I flagged a cab down and told him to drop me off at the emergency room on Jennifer Road. The funky ass African American cab was smelling like goat and dumpster juice. I didn't give a fuck though because I was in a life or death situation.

I passed out and when I woke up, I was in front of the Emergency room with the African pushing my shoulder yelling "Get out! I threw the five dollar bill at him and used all the strength that I had left to get out of the cab. As soon as the cab pulled off I passed out again and that's all I remember.

When I woke up I was in a hospital bed with two I.V's in my arm and my mother holding my hand crying. I looked at my mother and said,

"What are you crying for?"

She said, "You must like seeing me hurt don't you?"

I said, "Why would you say something like that"

She said, "Because you keep putting me through all this dumb shit. They bust my apartment over Eastport and found a scale".

I said, "I know, they already charged me with that".

She said, "They charged me too and what are they talking about that you had something to due with a murder?"

I said, "I don't know what they are talking about".

She said, "You're gonna keep on getting arrested until you get the message ain't you?

The door opened up and the doctor, Bossman and the flunky walked in. Doctor Reed was a sexy Spanish female that looked like Jennifer Lopez wearing some sexy glasses.

Bossman had the joker smile on his face and said,

"how you feeling lil Booh?"

With a deadly look on my face I responded,

"how the fuck you think I feel?"

My mother spoke up and said,

"watch your mouth boy!

That crack that I had swallowed had took it's toile on me. I was so dizzy and had a headache that was out this world.

Doctor Reed informed my mother that I had Over Dosed off of Crack Cocaine and that the amount that was in my blood system was so high that if I wouldn't have come to the hospital when I did that it would have been fatal.

Bossman spoke up and said,

"You swallowed some crack when we picked you up this morning didn't you?"

The flunky spoke up and said,

"I thought you looked strange".

My mother stared at me with this look on her face that I couldn't explain.

She said, "I know you ain't do no dumb shit like that?"

I looked at my mother, then looked at the Doctor and said,

"I was smoking crack that morning".

Bossman said, "He's lying. Doctor, can you pump his stomach out so that we can charge him with the drugs?" The look on my mother's face was a mixture of disappointment and terror that she almost lost her baby to drugs.

Doctor Redd said, "It's impossible at this point to pump his stomach because the cocaine is to far gone into the blood stream. What I'll do is have him drink a gallon of medicine that taste like chalk to help break down and get the Drug out of his system".

My mother asked her,

"Is my son going to be ok?"

Doctor Reed said, Let's see".

Doctor Reed looked at me and asked, "do you need to use the bathroom?"

I said, "Nawh".

She looked at my mother then said,

"I'm going to have to give your son a Cafether".

My mother said, "what's that?"

She said, "it's a procedure we do to help patients to Urinate".

I over heard the Doctor tell my mother that the Cocaine made me dehydrated, so she had to put fluid's into my body. That had been going on for about an hour now, so there's no reason why he shouldn't have to use the bathroom".

Doctor Reed looked at me with a serious look on her face and said,

"if you don't let me give you a cafether, your gonna die"

I said, "explain to me what your going to do".

She said, "during the procedure I would have to grab your penis and stick a Q-Tip down your urine whole and bust your Bladder".

With a disappointing look on my face I said,

"HELL NAWH!"

Doctor Reed pulled the Q-Tip out of her hospital jacket pocket and said,

"it's not gonna hurt, just don't look at it".

The Q-Tip was about 8" long. I didn't give a fuck how sexy Doctor Reed was, just the thought of her putting the Q-Tip down my penis hole was painful enough.

The whole time Bossman and the flunky had a smirk on their faces. I looked at the both of them and started calling them all types of Bitches, whores, motherfucka's etc . . . My mother begged me to calm down, it was like I was hearing her but I wasn't hearing her.

Doctor Reed said, "are y'all here to lock him up?"

Bossman said, "Nawh, we don't have a cause to lock him up".

Doctor Reed said, "Then I'm gonna have to ask ya'll to leave because he doesn't need to be upset in the condition that he's in".

Bossman looked at me and said,

"catch you later lil booh", while walking out the door.

Doctor Reed looked at me and said,

"are you ready?"

I said, "ain't no way that Q-Tip is going in my Dick!

My mother once again reminded me to watch my mouth. After I apologized, the Doctor looked at my mother and informed her that this procedure has to be done and that this was a life or death situation.

Doctor Reed said, "pull your hospital gown to the side Mr. Walders so that I can grab your penis and do my job".

I said, "ain't no way I'm going to do that".

She looked at me and said, "I didn't want to have to do this".

Doctor Reed said,

"Ms. Joan, can I speak to you in the hallway please?"

My mother looked at me and said,

"I'll be right back"

By the look on the Doctor's face, I knew she was up to something.

A couple of minutes had passed when the door opened and in came my mother, Doctor Reed and two "Big Ass" hospital security guards who both looked like bouncers at a night club.

I looked at my mother with a confused look on my face and said, "what's going on"

She said, "the security guards are here to hold you down while the Doctor does her job".

I said, "what"!

Before I knew it, the guards had both of my arms and legs pinned down, I was to weak to even try to fight with them. All I could do was curse and spit on them. My mother couldn't even watch, she quickly walked out of the room, while crying to herself. After putting the plastic gloves on, Doctor Reed grabbed my penis and told me don't look at it and that it'll all be over with soon. I closed my eyes and felt the Q-Tip go inside me, it was a painful feeling that I can't explain. When Doctor Reed busted my bladder, piss started shooting out everywhere. It felt like I was pissing for an hour. Doctor Reed held my penis in her hand so that the urine could go into the container that she had in her other hand. After the fluids drained out of my helpless body, I felt exhausted, all I wanted to do was get some sleep. The two guards finally unleashed me and walked out of the room. Doctor Reed went out in the hallway to get my mother. My mother came in while wiping her eyes and said,

"You alright?"

I said, "yeah, as long as you alright, then I'm alright."

Doctor Reed came in with a gallon of some shit that looked like motor oil. She informed us that this was the medicine that was going to help remove anymore cocaine that's in my system and that I had to drink the whole thing in an hour in order for it to work properly. The medicine tasted like chalk and left a bitter taste in my mouth. I was also informed by Doctor Reed that if I didn't drink it all with in the hour that I would have to start all over again. I wasn't trying to keep drinking that nasty shit all night so I forced myself and I finally finished in the proper amount of time. Every half an hour that went by, the chalky medicine had me shitting like crazy.

Doctor Reed informed my mother that I would have to be admitted to the hospital for a couple of days to make sure that I would be ok.

The days dragged on and on. All I could think about was that once again I cheated death, and all that money I was missing while I was being hospitalized.

I had a lot of visitors while I was in the hospital. My family members, Meka, Monique, Sherika, and some project girls came through also. After those couple of days passed, I was released to go home. Doctor Reed informed my mother that I would have to be on bed rest for about a week so that my brain and the rest of my body could return back to normal.

That whole week I stayed in the bed over at Eastport Terrace because I was still feeling dizzy. I had accepted the fact that nothing was certain, and that the "law of life" wasn't fixed. I realized that the best way to protect myself is to be as fluid and formless as water, because the situation that I just went through must never happen again. It's true what they say, "Once you experience a life or death situation you value your life more."

I had females waiting on me all day and night, my mother still came through every day after work to make sure I was alright.

Cheek-o came to holler at me to make sure I was alright and to inform me that Skip got locked up the other day. He said that Bossman and them busted his house down Bay Ridge and got a ½ brick of Powder Cocaine out of there. I was like, "Damn, just when shit was going good for me".

Cheek-o was from over Eastport and was Skips #2 man. Everybody always said that he looked like a shorter version of the rapper "Craig Mac."

Cheek-o said, "I got some information on a nigga name "Roosta" up Yankeeville (New York) that got some good pure Cocaine for a low price."

I said, "Yo, you crazy if you going "up top" to buy some Coke."

He said, "I talked to Eddie-D yesterday and he agreed to give us the Route, plus he could call Roosta up to let him know that we coming. Ain't nothing to it, and if we put our money together, that's more product for us".

I said, "I'll think about it."

He said, "I'm going up there in a couple of days with or without you." While walking out of my house he said, "money don't wait for nobody."

That night I thought long and hard at what Cheek-O told me. I remember Skip always saying, "either you in the game or in the way because the game never stops." I wanted to get that $100, 000 as soon as possible and keep my promise to my mother and him.

The next day I called Cheek-O and told him to meet me over my house later on and bring Eddie-D with him. They arrived at about 9:00 p.m.

Eddie-D was what we called an O.G. He's been putting in work for so long that he always liked to see other people doing it. It was rumored that when he was nineteen years old he killed his babies mother's brother, slit his throat over some money. Murder in the first is what the city of Annapolis gave him. He took the case to trial, Beat It, and ever since then he felt like he was undefeated. He always kept a tooth pick in his mouth and wore dark glasses even at night time. He loved to see young hustlers get money. He used to take trips back and forth up to Yankeeville for East Puerto-Ricans until about four months ago the word got back that the feds was on him.

"What's up Young Blood?"

I said, "ain't shit."

He said, "for future reference, don't you ever swallow no more crack because this game that we play ain't worth losing your life over . . . One way or another, you gotta respect the fact that life is a bitch and death is her twin sister, "They both go hand in hand."

I said, "I hear you, now let's get down to business."

Eddie-D said, "**Rule #1,** Y'all need to dress where as though ya'll look like some school kids and leave early in the morning about 5-5:30 a.m. so ya'll can get up B.W.I. (Baltimore Washington International) airport at the train station no later than 6:30 a.m., that's around the time kids catch the train to go to school. **Rule #2,** Don't buy your tickets at the same time, one of ya'll buy your ticket then the other buy theirs about 5 minutes later. That's so that the cameras don't see that ya'll are together. Make sure ya'll buy a one way ticket and never a round trip because that looks suspicious for two young black males to go up to N.Y. and back the same day. **Rule #3,** New York's Penn Station is ya'll stop. When ya'll get to the station be aware that there's a police area to your left after ya'll walk up the stairs. When ya'll walk out of Penn Station make a right to go to the subway. Make sure ya'll get on the train that's going uptown. Have some change for the toll fee.

Rule #4, Get off the train at 145th Broadway and Amsterdam, walk across the street down about a block to a restaurant with the Coca-Cola sign on it. Now, niggas gonna know ya'll ain't from up there, so they gonna be calling ya'll left and right trying to get ya'll to buy some cocaine from them. Pay them no mind, Roosta will have somebody meet ya'll at the restaurant.

Rule #5, Take an extra $500 so ya'll can go shopping while Roosta count ya'll money.

Rule #6, After ya'll buy the product, "Never" catch a cab from the spot because the D.E's (Drug enforcement's) be looking for suspicious shit like that. Catch the subway train back to Penn Station. Buy a one way ticket back to B.W.I. Airport.

Rule #7, Once ya'll back at the airport, "Don't" catch the cab back over Eastport because that looks to suspicious for two Hustling niggas getting out of an airport cab. Remember this shit young bloods like the back of your hand, because you don't want to write it down and risk having somebody find it". We went over the route and the rules Eddie-D told us until about midnight that night. We finally got it memorized. We both gave Eddie-D $500 a piece for giving us the road to success, because we knew that nothings for free.

Before Eddie-D left he said, "Don't get caught up in the games politics . . . stay far from Timid and only make moves when your hearts in it."

We decided that we were going to make the trip on the up coming Monday morning which was about four days away. That was good for us because we'll have time to buy the school clothes, and it'll give me a little more time to get my strength back from the overdose.

The thought crossed my mind many times that this could be my last time seeing Naptown, but "Fuck it" life was all about taking chances. If the game shakes me or breaks me, I hope that it makes me a better man. In Naptown the drug game needed change and I was the Cashier, nickel plated for the snitches, and I wanted Dime piece females laid in my bed.

I was cut from a different cloth, if Yankeeville was gonna make me be successful faster, "So be it!"

William James once said, "The greatest discovery of any generation is that a human being can alter their life by altering their attitude." My attitude was on a million, I had too much ambition for anybody to stop me!!!

Chapter 20

The Road to Success

Cheek-O and I caught a cab about 5:30 a.m. from over Eastport. Dressed in khakis, sweaters and soft shoes, nobody could tell that we were going up to Yankeeville to buy some cocaine.

When we got to the train station at B.W.I., Cheek-O bought his one way ticket then about five minutes later I bought mine. It was so many business and school people at the station that we blended right in.

After about 20 minutes the train came, we entered and sat right across from each other so that we could go over last minute things.

The energy that the business and school kids had on the train, you would've thought it was 3 o'clock in the afternoon.

This was our first time on a train, so we were looking out the window the whole time, like we were on a field trip.

Our first stop was Baltimore Penn Station. The station was raggedy and had a smell of death to it, for all I knew it could've been a dead body somewhere down by the tracks.

Our next stop was Philly, to our surprise the row houses and street's looked just like Baltimore.

Newark was next, then came New Jersey, then finally came "The Rotten Apple (N.Y.)

New York is the gateway to the United States, says most of the immigrants from different countries. The land of opportunity, they call it. It's also the home of the largest stock exchange in the U.S. and also the cocaine capital of the east coast. One could come over and live the "American Dream." For example, look at the movie, "Scarface". Tony was a poor Cuban who came to the U.S. and became one of the Biggest Drug Dealers that the so called "Land of the free" had ever seen.

The train ride took about two and a half hours but it seemed longer. When the person on the loud speaker said, "last stop New York's Penn Station," the train stopped. I looked at Cheek-O and said, "ain't no turning back now."

He said, "I know."

It was so many people at Penn station that you had to bump and rub shoulders to get past.

Just like Eddie-D told us, there was a police area to the left with about 8-10 officer's looking for suspicious people and acts.

Outside of the station looked like something off of a movie. Everybody looked as though they had something to do or somewhere to be.

Yankeeville was way faster than where I was from. It brought me to the reality that it wouldn't take no more than a N.Y. minute for one of these niggas to take our money and put a bullet in our head. Just the thought of my body getting sent to my mother in a box kept me focused and on point in the city that never sleeps.

We walked down to the subway and paid the toll fee to go to "Broadway and Amsterdam." The train smelled like piss and the bums who used it for shelter didn't help the aroma either. We got off on 145th and walked across the street to look for the restaurant with the Coca-Cola sign on it. Soon as we stepped foot on the side walk you would've thought that we had a sign on our head that read "we want to buy some cocaine" the way niggas was trying to pull us up. "Poppy I got that butter, poppy low prices," that's all they was saying. We paid them no mind and kept it moving about two blocks down the street where we found the Coca-Cola sign. When we walked into the restaurant I was glad to be off of the radar of Manhattan, it seemed like the whole New York was watching us.

The restaurant smelled like fried vegetables and sausage. A Spanish boy walked towards us and introduced himself as Rick.

Rick said, "Maryland, Maryland."

Me and Cheek-O looked at each other and I said, "yeah we from Maryland and we here to see a Roosta." Rick smiled and said, "Roosta yes, come ... come." We followed Rick about two blocks down the street to an apartment building, Niggas was crowded out front of this building steps just like any other project building. Rick said something in Spanish to them and they cleared the path for us to pass. I just so happened to look up and see niggas on the roof with walkie talkies to their mouths. I thought to myself, "Damn, Poppy is real organized up here."

The building smelled like old piss and fried vegetables. Rick walked us to the third floor and knocked on the door three times. A sexy ass Spanish girl who looked like Eva Mendez opened the door with just a towel on and half her hair in a pony tail. From looking at how wet her hair and body was you could tell she just got out the shower. Rick said something to her in Spanish then pointed at me and Cheek-O and said, "Maryland." The Spanish butterfly opened the door all the way and let us in. When I passed her, she and I made eye contact and she gave me a smile with her sexy lips.

Rick spoke to her in Spanish, she translated to us informing us that Roosta will be here in a couple of minutes.

Cheek-O said, "What's your name?"

She said, "Tina."

Tina was bad, plus she had some sexy feet.

She smiled at me and said,

"I'm going to put some clothes on."

Rick just stared at me and smiled, he knew I wanted to fuck her. I came back to reality because I knew that it wasn't that type of party, we weren't there for pleasure it was for business.

The scenery looked exactly like the one on "Scarface" when Tony went to meet the Colombians. The small black and white T.V. was blurry and had Spanish people talking on it.

Tina came back in after a couple of minutes wearing some boy shorts that hugged her ass and with a tank top on that showed her nipples because she had no bra on.

Cheek-O said, "Tina, can you tell Rick to go get us something to eat at the restaurant down the street?"

I knew where Cheek-O's mind was, he wanted to fuck Tina also."

Tina spoke in Spanish to Rick.

Rick said, "yeah, yeah."

I gave Rick $20.00 and told Tina to tell him to bring us some burgers, fries and something to drink. I was so focused on this trip that I hadn't even thought about eating this morning. Tina spoke in Spanish to Rick again and he smiled at us and walked out the door.

Cheek-O asked Tina, "how did you learn to speak English?"

Tina said, "I came to New York when I was 3 years old and went to a regular school."

Cheek-O said, "You got a man?"

Tina told him no then she smiled at me. I asked Tina had she ever been to Maryland before and she said no.

I said, "Maybe I can make that happen for you."

She smiled.

When I heard the door open up I said to myself, "Damn I know that nigga Rick ain't back that fast, just when I was getting my rap on." A guy came walking through the door eating a sandwich. Tina spoke in Spanish to him, at the end of their sentence she said, "Maryland."

The guy walked over to us and extended his hand to greet us.

He said, "I'm Roosta."

Roosta looked like "lu-lu" off of the "Paid In Full" movie. We both shook his hand and introduced ourselves. Roosta pulled up a chair then said,

"Eddie-D called, I've been expecting you . . . how was the trip?"

Cheek-O said, "Long."

Roosta said, "I hope my niece kept you company."

I said, "yeah, she did."

Tina looked at me and smiled.

There was three knocks at the door, Roosta looked at Tina and signaled her to get it. Rick walked in with two bags of food, three sodas and sat it on the kitchen table.

Roosta looked at us and said,

"how much ya'll trying to spend?"

Cheek-O said, "what's the #'s looking like?"

Roosta leaned back in the chair and said,

"$18 a gram."

I knew in Hustling words that meant $18,000 a Kilo. We had $14,000 a piece, we could buy a brick and a ½ of pure cocaine, plus put $500 back in our pocket. Cheek-O looked at me, then looked at Roosta and said, "we want a brick and a half."

Roosta smiled, then said,

"that's why I love Maryland."

I took my money out my book bag and put it on the coffee table, so did Cheek-O. We both made sure that we took out the extra $500 because we both needed that.

Roosta informed us that he was going to count the money then call for the cocaine to come.

Cheek-O said, "You ain't gotta count it cause it's all there poppy."

I said, "how long?"

Roosta said, "1/2 hour . . . in the mean time Rick gonna take ya'll to the store to go buy a couple of things, and when ya'll come back it'll be here." Me and Cheek-O both said, "alright."

Roosta spoke to Rick in Spanish, after he was done Rick looked at us then said,

"Yeah . . . come, come."

While he was walking out the door, I looked at Tina and said,

"I'll be right back."

She smiled.

Rick flagged a cab down and we were taken to the foot locker on 125th street. The cab driver was a skinny African that looked like Smokie on the old cartoons "The P.J's." The cab ride was not long, but the smell of goat and under arms made it seem like it was for hours.

That was the first time I got a look at Harlem. I used to see movies that had scenes of it, but it wasn't anything compared to seeing it first hand. Harlem was "fucked up." It looked like somebody dropped a bomb on it.

We bought a couple of pairs of Jordan's that we never saw before, it was true what they say that Yankeeville always got the new shoes first.

We got back to 145th street about an hour later. After getting to the third floor and Rick knocking three times on the door, Tina opened up and let us in. She looked at me and said,

"You buy me something?"

I said, "When I bring you to Maryland I'm going to buy you something."

She shut the door behind me and said,

"I didn't know I was planning a trip to Maryland?"

I smiled then said, "Now you do."

Roosta smiled then signaled me to sit on the couch next to Cheek-O.

He said, "I counted out $27,000 and the product is on the way."

I thought to myself, "Damn, it's about 3pm now . . . by the time we get back to Naptown it'll be later on tonight." By the look on Cheek-O face, I could tell he was thinking the same thing. Roosta saw the expressions on our faces and said,

"Don't worry, it's on the way."

After Roosta made that comment there was another knock at the door. Roosta smiled at us then signaled Tina to get it. The person who walked in looked and smelled like an old street bum. He gave Tina a brown grocery paper bag and then walked back out of the apartment. After shutting the door she handed the bag to Roosta. He told Tina to get the scale in the kitchen drawer. In the grocery bag, Roosta pulled out two big ass bags full with pure cocaine. He put the bags on the table in front of us then said,

"Good cocaine," while smiling. Me and Cheek-O's eyes widened up because we had never seen that much cocaine before. The smell was so strong that a police dog could've smelled it a mile away.

It was at that moment in my life that I seriously said to myself, "nigga you ready to get paid."

Tina put a big ass triple beam scale on the table. Roosta put both bags on the scale separately and they both read 750 grams a piece. He looked at us then said,

"a kilo and a half of pure cocaine."

Cheek-O said, "that's what's up."

Roosta told Tina to get the duck tape so that he could try to cover up some of the smell. After he taped each bag up real tight, he handed them to us, then we put them in our book bags.

Roosta gave both of us his # and said,

"anytime ya'll want good coke, call me"

I took two deep breaths, one was for buying the product successfully and the other was for the upcoming obstacles that the long ride back to Naptown had in store for us.

Cheek-O said, "we'll call you next week to come back to holla at you."

Roosta spoke Spanish to Rick then he looked at us, then said,

"Rick gonna make sure ya'll get on the subway safely."

We both said, "alright."

After shaking Roostas hand, we both walked towards the door with Tina leading. When I got to the door I said,

"Tina you gonna be here when I come back?"

She held her hand out with a phone # on a piece of paper and said,

"call me when you get some free time."

I took the # with a cool-aid smile on my face and said,

"I'ma do that."

Cheek-O and Rick looked at me and started smiling.

When we got to the subway I reminded Cheek-O that Eddie-D said don't buy our tickets at the same time. After I bought my ticket, I saw a crowd of school kids going towards our destination so I just blended right in with them. The police at the security area paid me no mind. I guess they wouldn't suspect school kids to be carrying cocaine on them. Cheek-O came down the steps about 5 minutes later.

I said, "you alright?"

He said, "yeah., the police never looked in my direction."

The train came about 20 minutes later. As soon as we got seated, I told Cheek-O to wake me up when we got close to Baltimore, then I went out like a light.

It seemed like as soon as I closed my eyes, Cheek-O was pushing my shoulder telling me "get up." When I got up I looked out the window then asked Cheek-O,

"Do everything look alright?"

He said, "yeah, nothing don't look strange."

There was no police or detectives in sight.

At the train station in Baltimore, we caught a cab down to Naptown. The fat ass cab driver who looked like "Fat Albert," made the ride uncomfortable for us. He kept asking us questions like were we on trial.

Fat Albert said, "where ya'll from out of town?"

I said, "Nawh, we go to school in Maryland."

He said, "why ya'll catching a cab from the train station?"

Cheek-O spoke up and said,

"look nigga, we paying you to take us to Annapolis so stop with all the fucking questions!"

Fat Albert said, "Sorry man, I'm just trying to make conversation."

I whispered to Cheek-O

"Chill yo, I don't think he meant nothing by it."

When we got to the Annapolis Mall I gave the cab driver a $100 and told him to keep the change. Once we were out of sight of the cab driver, we gave each other a brotherly hug. The expression on our faces showed that we were glad that we made a successful trip and that we were back in Naptown.

Chapter 21

Against All Odds

Eighteen months had passed and a lot of things had changed. My mother and I went to court for the house raid, it only took Peter O'Neel 5 minutes in court to get the case dismissed due to the fact that the warrant was for a murder weapon and not a scale. Housing Authority still took my mother's place from her, even though the case got thrown out because they said that I was considered a public nuisance. My mother wasn't mad about it though, I guess she felt as though if I wasn't living over Eastport than maybe I would stop selling drugs.

I stayed out Allen's apartment with my mother and her boyfriend for about a month until my uncle and I got an apartment together down at Forest Village. "Broad" spent most of his time in V.A. over his girlfriend's house so I didn't have to worry about him being in my way.

Now that I was no longer a residence over at Eastport, Bossman had probable cause to lock me up for trespassing. The five trespassing charges that I received for being on Housing authority property, O'Neel got them consolidated and I coped-out to 5 years probation.

Judge Grean was a known black judge in Annapolis, the way he was hanging niggas you would've thought he was white. He told me that if I was ever found guilty again, that I was going to prison. I wasn't paying him any mind though. I was back over Eastport that same day. I was getting a lot of money, I felt invincible.

The one thing that didn't change was that Cheek-O and I were back and forth up to Yankeeville every Monday, sometimes twice a week.

Between my cousin-C down in the county, and niggas over Eastport, it ain't take me any time to get rid of the cocaine I brought back.

We started buying so much weight that we had to take Bowsky up to Yankeeville with us to help bring some back. Bowsky was one of our neighborhood crack heads that was willing to take the trip with us for an once of crack every time. That nigga would have so much cocaine tapped to his body that you would've mistaken him for a "suicide bomber."

I graduated from high school with honors. My mother and the rest of the family were so proud of me. To treat myself I decided to buy my first car. I didn't even have a license. All them Rental rocks that I was paying to drive around in, I figured it would be cheaper to buy my own car. An old Naptown veteran cab driver named Russ put me down with an auction in Delaware and agreed to take me there for a small fee.

I spent $1,000 on a green 1968 Plymouth Fury 3', and drove it back to Naptown with bad tags on it, while Russ followed behind me. My mother told me that the only way she would put the car in her name is if I got my license.

I paid for the $400 class and it only took me a little over a month to get my license. I had already taught myself how to be a good driver by using the crack heads cars as learning guides

I tinted the windows, put a $800 stereo system in it and threw some 20" Dayton rims on the wheels to make it official. I was driving around Naptown like I was in L.A. Everybody loved my car, everywhere I went heads turned, white or black. Niggas loved it so much that they started buying old cars and hooking them up. "Fuck it though," people just loved my swagga and they knew I was the type of person to do shit ordinary niggas wouldn't do.

I felt like I was on top of the world, nobody couldn't tell me anything. Hate it or love it, the underdog was finally on top.

My pussy rate went sky high and more importantly my money was right.

Every chance I got I would go up to the Geavonie store up in Georgetown, to buy some clothes. The owner remembered my face from coming to the store so much that he would always give me discounts. After spending no less than $500 every time, he would send me across the street to the Chinese woman so that she could tailor my linen for me right then and there.

I'd go to "Club Hollywood" in Naptown shining. I was wearing Versace, silk shirts, linen pants and all types of gator shoes. On celebrity

Sundays, I'd pay a $100 at the door because I was only 17 years old at the time.

About three months from when I first saw Tina, I brought her to Maryland and got us a room at the "Four Seasons Hotel" in D.C., she was worth it. Tina informed me that she was in college to get her masters degree in psychology and that the only reason that she's involved with her cousin Roosta's life style is because he pays for everything for her.

There's nothing more sexy than a woman that wants, but don't need me.

The Four Seasons Hotel was lovely. The $900 a night room would've made anybody feel like a King or Queen.

We have been talking on the phone almost every day since we first met. It was new to me, knowing that I could have a relationship with a female for a period of time without even having sex with her yet. She always bragged to me about how good she thought her sex was and how I was gonna be whipped.

Inside the room, Tina didn't waste anytime to show me how much she liked me. She pushed me on the bed and started to strip me naked. My dick got hard instantly, it laid on my stomach like a baby anaconda. She tried to be discrete and not let me see her look at it, but it was obvious the way she smiled and licked her lips. Once my clothes were off, she stood on the side of the bed and started getting naked while smiling and looking in my eyes.

The Four Seasons Hotel bed was so soft it looked like I was sinking in it.

After Tina was completely naked, I just stared at her and observed how beautiful her body was. She was a dime anyway, but her body looked like God broke the mold when he made her. Her breast stood firm while her long pretty hair came just to her nipples. Her nicely petite six pack, which you can barely see when she turned to the side, made her thighs spread out like they were trying to swallow her completely shaved pussy, which had a gap below it the size of a quarter. Tina Smiled at me then said,

"You like what you see poppy?"

"Hell yeah!" I replied.

She looked at my dick then said,

`"I can tell."

Tina pressed play on the stereo and Mary J Blige started singing "Share my world." Before I knew it, she jumped on the bed with her legs spread over top of me, hands on her hips and slowly started dancing. I was on cloud nine and I haven't even got into the pussy yet. While Mary J Blige sung to us, Tina danced away and my eyes stayed wide open because I didn't want to miss any moment of the show she was giving me. My dick jumped up then slammed back on my stomach repeatedly.

After having me hypnotize by looking at her hips for about five minutes, Tina slowly laid her body on mine. She whispered in my ear,

"you ready for this pussy poppy?"

I said, "I been ready since the first time I saw you."

While Tina slowly kissed on my face, she used her right hand to slowly guide my dick into her tight wet pussy. I could tell that she hadn't had sex in a while because for about five minutes all she did was guide my dick through her wet walls slowly in a circular motion.

Normally in a situation like this I would've beat the pussy up, but it was different with Tina. I think that was the first time in my life that I really was in love. When I was fourteen, I thought I was in love with Nickeana from Philly, but now I had realized that was just puppy love.

To me, Tina was definitely an angel who fell from heaven. For that reason alone, I just sat back and enjoyed the moment. Once she had half of my dick inside her, she stopped and continued to kiss on me. I started kissing behind her ear, it must have been her spot because she started to move her hips up and down. The more she moved and scratched my shoulders, the tighter I squeezed her apple ass. The whole hour that Mary J Blige sung to us, Tina never missed a beat. The King size bed was so wet from all the multiple orgasms she had, I thought that she had pissed on me.

That was the first time that I had ever made love, and believe me "that shit felt good." It also was the first time that I had sex and didn't have to do any work, if you think about it, you could say that she fucked the shit out of me.

We constantly made love that whole night at the Four Seasons Hotel. I felt like the President of the United States and Tina was the first lady. She warned me that when I got the pussy that I was gonna be whipped, she was right!!

I took Tina to Tyson's Corner, Pentagon City and George Town to go shopping, every time she came to Maryland to visit me, because she wasn't the type of female that you took to Annapolis Mall.

Whenever I took her over to Eastport, all the Project Bitch's would hate on her, and the niggas would practically drewl from their mouths. She had me feeling like my daddy back in the 80's, my love was without a limit with her.

Tina definitely had me thinking about life more seriously, she had a nigga "Wide Open".

Everything was going good until that day when Bossman & the flunky came on foot and locked me up over at Eastport Terrace while I was sitting on my car. After getting the usual harassment from them, I received a $30,000 bail from the commissioner for trespassing on Housing Authority Property. I got Pack-O to come bail me out before they took me to the Detention Center, it was no problem for him because he knew my money was good.

About a month later, Pack-O informed me that I had a Probation Violation warrant on me with a $30,000 bail. I told O'Neel about it and he told me to turn myself in and if I didn't get bail then he'd be at my bail hearing. I did, I got bail so Pack-O came and bailed me out and I was back over Eastport later that day.

I went to see O'Neel the next day and he informed me that the Violation of Probation was for trespassing and that it was gonna be up to the judge for the out come of it. Peter also requested that if I give him a $1,000 he'll talk to the prosecutor about the case, but he also said "no promises". I agreed.

My court date was September 12th at 9a.m. I had to tell Tina that it was a possibility that I was going to jail for a little while. O'Neel (Superman) couldn't save me this time, Judge Grean had the Kryptonite to stop him and he had it out for my ass.

I called Tina and told her that I had to talk to her in person about something important.

She knew something was wrong.

She said, "if it's bad news then tell me now".

I refused to tell her over the phone, so I said.

"I holler at you when Cheek-O, Charles and me make the trip on Monday".

Before hanging the phone up she told me that she loved me and that she'll see me in a couple days.

We got off of the subway on a 145th street and to our surprise the whole block was packed with cops and the ambulance. Rick was at the restaurant as usual waiting for us, but this time he had a female with him, who looked like she was about 14 teen yrs old. Rick walked over to us with a strange look on his face.

He said, "Maryland, Maryland".

He greeted us with a hand shake but this time he didn't give us his usual smile.

Cheek-O pointed outside the restaurant then said,

"what happened?"

Rick spoke Spanish to the female, she looked at us then said, "Rick said that Roosta and Tina got killed".

I said, "what!"

She said, "some niggas from Brooklyn came through and ran up in the spot".

With rage in my blood I said,

"How the fuck could that happen when Roosta had niggas outside on the roof!"

She translated it to Rick, after he spoke back to her in Spanish she said,

"two niggas went into the apartment like they was buying some kilo's, once they got in they walkie talkied their soldiers to come in . . . it was a shoot out in the middle of the street, three niggas from Brooklyn got killed but the rest got away . . . when the police got to the apartment, they found Roosta and Tina both shot execution style in the back of their heads".

I sat there and thought to myself "Danm, I really had caught feelings for Tina and now she was gone".

Tina wasn't like your average project chick. She was trying to be something in life. Even though she was involved in the drug game, she still didn't deserve to die like that. On the other hand in Roosta's situation, you had to charge that to the game.

Cheek-O asked the girl.

"Ask Rick do he know somebody else who got some good cocaine".

After she spoke to Rick and he spoke back to her she told Cheek-O,

"Rick said that Randy got the same Coke like Roosta had".

Cheek-O looked at me then said,

"Yo, I know you fucked up with the situation about Tina . . . but you know we came up here for business".

It showed that I was hurting bad inside but he was right, I had to get myself together, it'll be plenty of time for me to mourn over Tina.

I looked at Cheek-O then said,

"lets do it".

Cheek-O said, "that's what I'm talking about". He then looked at the girl and said,

"tell Rick to take us to Randy".

She did.

Rick guided us down 141st street to this sub restaurant that had the smell of onions and fried steak. Although the aroma made me hungry I couldn't eat at that moment because I was still thinking about Tina.

We sat down at the table while Rick went to the counter to talk to the cook.

I asked the girl, "did Tina have more family over here so that I could send them money to help with the funeral".

She said, "Besides Roosta, the rest of her family is back in Puerto Rico".

I felt bad knowing that I couldn't do anything to help with Tina's situation. Rick walked back over and spoke Spanish to the girl. She told us that Randy would be here in a couple of minutes. Rick stared and smiled at us the whole time.

Cheek-O said, "I'm going get something to eat", Bowsky followed behind him.

After a couple of minutes, a tall brown skin Dominican walked in. After Rick spoke Spanish to him, he walked over to us and extended his hand to me and said, "Maryland."

I shook his hand and said,

"Yeah".

When Cheek-O and Bowsky came over with their food, the guy greeted them the same way. He introduced himself as "Logo" and told us that he was going take us to Randy.

A block over and down the street was where he led us to a hair salon. He walked us to the back of the empty shop into the bathroom. At the empty stool he banged on the wall four times and the wall opened up. I said to myself, "Damn Poppy got the same shit the government got. In the small room, was a table and four chairs.

Logo said, "have a seat, Randy will be here in a minute".

At no time did I ever get used to going up to N.Y. to buy some cocaine, all this shit up here was a death trap. I guess that was the chance niggas was willing to take to live the American Dream.

After a couple of minutes a short stocky dark skin nigga walked in and spoke Spanish to Logo, then he looked at us and said,

"Maryland".

After he greeted us with a hand shake,

He said, "I'm Randy, I'm sorry to here about what happened to Roosta and his cousin."

After giving his condolences, Randy wasted no time getting down to business.

He said, "how much cocaine".

Cheek-O said, "what's the #'s?"

"$18 a gram", Randy replied.

I said, "we want four bricks and how long is it gonna take to get here?"

I was trying to get the fuck out of N.Y. as soon as possible.

Randy said, "give me one second".

He pulled a walkie talkie out of his pocket and spoke Spanish to it. The person on the other end said,

"Ok".

Randy said, "By the time I finish counting the money it'll be here".

I pulled the $36,000 out of my book bag and sat it on the table, Cheek-O followed suit. We all sat quietly while Randy counted the money. A couple of seconds after he approved that it was $72,000 the back door opened up. To my surprise, the same bum that brought Roosta his package was the same one bringing Randy his. After giving Randy a brown paper grocery bag, he received a couple of dollars and was sent on his way. While smiling, Randy pulled out a triple beam scale and four big ass zip-lock bags filled with cocaine. The coke was so strong that we smelled it as soon as it came into the room.

One by one Randy dropped the zip-lock bags on the scale which all of them red 1000 grams. Randy then pulled out some duck tape and began to tape up the product.

I said, "Bowsky, strip down to your boxers so we can tape the weight on to you so that we can hurry up and get the fuck out here".

After Bowsky undressed, Cheek-O and me duck taped a kilo to each of his arms, and a kilo to each of his legs. Everybody else that was in the room looked at us like we were crazy. After we finished, Randy wrote down his # and told us to call him when we were ready to come back to see him.

Rick walked us back to the subway and waited with us until the train came. We knew that this was probably going to be our last time seeing Rick, so we gave him $500 a piece and a brotherly hug before we left.

When we got back to Naptown, I didn't even tamper with the two bricks. It was about 10:30 p.m. when I got to my apartment at Forest Village. All I could do was lay in my bed and think about Tina, I was sure that we had a promising future in our relationship. I guess that's what I get for wishful thinking. I knew that Tina was going to be irreplaceable.

I had to cut my phone off because niggas kept blowing it up trying to buy some work. I was tired, not physically but mentally. The drug game was taking its toll on me. Between running back and fourth up to N.Y. and my upcoming court date, I was "exhausted". It was at that time that I decided that I wasn't going back to Yankeeville until after my upcoming court date.

C h a p t e r   2 2

If Your Not Part of The Solution, Your Part of The Problem

The dispatcher at the Annapolis cab company sent word over to Eastport to Eddie-D to let us know that the F.E.D's had come around and started asking questions about trips that were being made back and forth to B.W.I airport. Cheek-O didn't care though, he just started trying to find a different way to get up to N.Y. I was satisfied though, my mind was made up after that last trip.

The last couple of days all I did was party with bitches and lay around looking stupid.

March 8th seemed like it came so fast. The day before I went to court, I got Sherica to put dread-locks in my hair, she was from over Eastport. She and I had been fucking around every now and then, nothing serious because I was to busy living the street life. I figured if I had to do some prison time I didn't want to have my hair all nappy, plus with dreads all I had to do is twist it up myself.

My mother and I met Mr. O'Neel outside of the courtroom, he greeted us with the usual hand shake.

O'Neel said, "so since it's up to the judge, it's still a good possibility that he's going to jail?"

O'Neel put his arm around my mother then said,

"its up to the judge Ms. Joan".

"All rise! The bailiff shouted.

Judge Grean walked in and said

"you may be seated".

"State v.s Rome Walders Jr, for Violation of Probation," the Britney Spears look alike prosecutor said.

Judge Grean looked at his court papers then looked at Mr.O'Neel and said,

"you have anything to say?"

O'Neel said, "your honor, my client filed harassment charges on the officer's that had locked him up for this charge" Judge Grean interrupted and said,

"this incident happened on Housing Authority Property?"

O'Neel said, "it did your honor".

Judge Grean said, "Mr.Walders, didn't I tell you that I didn't want you to go back on the property?"

I said, "I got family over there, I'm not breaking any laws on Housing Authority Property".

O'Neel spoke up and said,

"your Honor my client at no time has broken any laws on the property".

Judge Grean said, "yeah, except for being on it . . . does the prosecutor have anything to say?"

She said, "whatever decision you make is ok with me your honor".

✶ ⌜Judge Green said, "Mr.Walders, I am going to sentence you to 5 yrs at D.O.C(Division of Corrections) for the Violation of Probation.⌝I heard my mother in the back ground crying to herself. I looked back to see the expression on Bossman's face, the smile that was on his and the flunky's face showed that they were satisfied with the judges decision.

The bailiff told me to put my hands behind my back. My mother asked Mr. O'Neel,

"would my son be doing his time at the Detention Center?"

Mr. O'Neel said, "he'll be at the center for a couple of days then he'll be transferred to Baltimore at the D.O.C so that they can prepare him for prison".

My mother walked over and gave me a hug, kiss and told me to call as soon as I could. I really wasn't worried about the sentence, but what really was hurting me was seeing my mother crying once again over something that I've done. I told her don't worry about me, I'll be ok. Mr. O'Neel told us that he thought that the sentence was Harsh and that he was going to put in a modification of the sentence.

✶⌜Since I was 18yrs old now, they put me in general population. I practically knew everybody down their. Word had traveled fast that I had gotten 5yrs for Violation of Probation. Detention Center was a war zone for a lot of inmates. Niggas from different projects in Naptown, who was at war on the streets used the Center as a killing field. Pioneer City, Meadvillage, FreeTown, D.C and Baltimore was prey to the Naptown Niggas.

My father was also at the jail but was on a different tier. When he got word that his son was upstairs, he asked the captain could she arrange a meeting between the both of us before I went to D.O.C, she agreed. A couple of days later the C.O took me to a small room that the facility used for attorney visits to let me and my father talk for an hour.

My father looked good, the 5 months he had been locked up I could tell that the money I had been sending had him eating good at the jail. I still could see that he tried to hide the hurt in his face with smiles while we talked.

He said, "I feel like it's my fault that your in the situation your in".

I said, "I am a grown man, I made my bed so now I have to lay in it".

My father was no stranger to doing time, so he gave me as much knowledge as he could before the C.O cut our visit short because [RobinWood niggas started beefing with Annapolis Gardens Boys on the steel side. The most important thing he told me was "don't take shit from anybody, if a nigga wanted it then give it to him and don't play around when you do".]

I appreciate my father trying to give me a heads-up on what I was about to face, but I had already learned how to move in a room full of vultures. If you were in the position that I was in on the streets, you learned it one way or another.

Before leaving he gave me a long tight fatherly hug and told me he loved me. I told him the same as well.

A couple of days later they had me and four other inmates chained and shackled on a D.O.C. bus on our way to Baltimore. The ride to the city was about 40 minutes long but it felt longer because I didn't know what to expect.

[After entering the D.O.C building we all got on an elevator with another C.O., who looked like the singer Ashanti, she took us to the 5th floor. Sexy Ashanti's job was to transport inmates up and down the elevator for 8 hours a day.]

After getting off the elevator, the C.O. put us in a holding tank with a T.V. that had the wheel of fortune on it.

After an hour had passed, we all were called one by one to strip ass naked and to take a shower. We were given institutional jeans, shirt and a New Man Package. After our picture was taken and asked what seemed like a million and one questions, they allowed us to make a 5 minute phone call. I called out Bestgates hoping that my mother was there. My grandmother answered the phone and informed me that my mother hadn't gotten back from work yet. I couldn't stay on the phone and wait for her so I told my grandmother that I would call back tomorrow around the same time. Before I hung up the phone she said that she loved me and that she was praying for me, I told her that I loved her also.

After everybody used the phone the C.O. took us to the 2nd floor where we observed some guys walking by wearing burgundy jump suits. One of the inmates who was in my group asked the C.O. what they were wearing them jump suits for. The C.O. said that they were federal inmates, ya'll definitely don't want to go where they going. When we got to our tier all the other inmates were locked in their cells. Ms. Jones was the C.O. who ran the tier. She was a real big Kelly Price looking female but with a cuter face. She informed us that we would get to use the phone today at 7-9 when we come out for recreation and tomorrow we'll come out at 1-3 p.m. It was about 12 o'clock so I had about 7 hours until I got to use the phone. Ms. Jones started calling off our names and giving us the cell #'s where we would be staying.

I was put into a cell with a dope fiend. Nigga named Tony, who was going through withdrawals. He looked like he was 40yrs old but told me he was 23. The streets had taken Tony's appearance and deflated his weight like a true fiend. I had the top bunk so I laid back and tried to get some rest before we went out for recreation. Tony didn't have much talk for me because he was to busy throwing up and shitting on himself. The only good thing about being in the cell with a dope fiend was that he gave me all of his food because he was to ill to eat.

When we finally got to use the phone, I talked to my mother and informed her that I was ok. The 5 minute call went so fast. I had to call back at least 6 more times to get a good conversation. I let her know that hopefully I'll get sent to somewhere close to home, that way she'd be able to come and see me when she wanted to.

C h a p t e r   2 3

Jessup State Correctional Facility

The month that I stayed down at the D.O.C was exhausting. Between being treated like a research monkey while going through the medical procedure's and Tony getting on my fucking nerves, I was ready for the State System.

After I was classified, the counselor informed me that my designation was going to be Jessup, Maryland.

★ [Brockbridge was a battle field because it was a transit spot, you might get inmates going to a maximum prison or you might get some going down to a prerelease prison.

★[Brockbridge has 8 Dorms downstairs and 8 dorms upstairs. At 10 o'clock, the C.O's lock the cages and are suppose to make their rounds every hour which they don't. The dorms were all death traps. 75 inmates stayed in each cage with 3 bathrooms, 3 showers, one T.V and two big ass fans in the front of the block.[Everybody Monday thru Friday at 6 o'clock pm, every inmate in the dorm would have their eye's looking at 106 & Park hoping that "Free" would have some tight ass jeans on her phat ass.

When I stepped foot into the dorm, it was people everywhere. As soon as I put my institutional package on my bunk, three niggas came in with pillow cases on their heads and robbed and stabbed another inmate in the front of the dorm. I was like, "damn, that shit happened so fast". By the time the C.O's came, the person who got stabbed was laying in a pool of his own blood. When I saw that his eyes was wide open, I knew he was dead. We were locked down for a week for that situation, but that was far from being the last.

[I stayed at Brockbridge for six months, in those months I witnessed stabbings, robberies and many other assaults. I also witnessed inmates chasing faggots all day and night. In any penal or federal system, it didn't matter if you were 3-8 feet tall. If you could lift every weight in the prison, if you were skin and bones, because that knife would easily size any inmate-up.]

We got to see movies every weekend, Friday was known as "Freaky Friday", because that movie for that night was going to be on a pornography level. A nigga from out of D.C couldn't help himself and ended up raping a Chinese boy in the shower, that was the end of Freaky Friday.

[Brockbridge was in a world of its own. From there, I was destined to J.P.R.U (Jessup Pre-Release Unit). My first reaction to the facility was that it reminded me of being down the country because of the trailers that they used as dorms. The police bubble connected two trailers together which both sides had about 70 inmates a piece in each dorm.

[J.R.U was a prerelease facility, so it wasn't anywhere near as violent as Brockbridge, but don't get it twisted because shit still happened.

It was like I was on the streets at J.P.R.U because the $85 you could have in your pocket made it easier for the young C.O bitches to fuck, suck and break any and every law possible that they could.]

Inmates would walk around the track smoking blunts, white boys would be in the cut by the volleyball court smoking crack and the dope fiends would be snorting and shooting dope in their veins at any blind spot in the prison they could find.

Instead of some of the inmates paying the female staff to bring in drugs for them, they would rather get love ones to drive on the side of the prison like they were going to the gun range and throw the work over the fence.

I became cool with a lot of Baltimore niggas when I was down J.P.R.U. One thing I realized is that most of the Baltimoreans would rather be cool with a county person then someone from their city because Baltimore was so corrupt.

I also got cool with a nigga from Cambridge, name Ron. He and I use to stay up half the night and compare our hoods to each other. I used to laugh at him all the time about his country accent. He was sentenced to 5 yrs for serving an undercover a $10 crack rock. He was from [Cambridge and I knew there was a lot of money down there cause Jay-Z always talked about it.]

He said, "off an Ounce of crack I could make about $2,500"

I said, "Damn!"

He said, "the flip side of getting so much more money is that you get caught selling any drugs, it's a good chance that you could get sentenced to double digits. Yankee (N.Y.) niggas be coming down there and selling ounces for $1,000 a piece and those were good prices".

I said, "when we get home would you be willing to come across the Bay Bridge to Naptown and holler at me?"

He said, "what's the #'s?"

I said, "I give it to you for $800 an ounce and the product is gonna be good".

He said, "hell yeah!"

✳ [The next day I called my brother to see what was up with him. Black informed me that my comrade "Killa" got slumped over Eastport the other day.] He also told me that half got 10 yrs up Hagerstown, Riley was still acting out, and niggas was still beefing with each other down Naptown hard. When I got off of the phone with him, I went to my bunk and stayed there for the rest of the day, thinking about "Killa." He was like a brother to me. Life was crazy like that sometimes. It's true when they say that you never really miss someone until they're gone.

After about a couple of years, my cousin's father (big-H) came to J.P.R.U. He was real popular at "the cut" (Maryland House of Corrections). It was called "the Cut" because of the violent acts that occurred at the prison. Me along with the other J.P.R.U inmates use to watch from the yard and witness how the helicopter would land in the killing field to fly an inmate up out of there, who just got chopped up. Niggas use to bet money with each other if the inmate would live or die. The way you would find out if the person possibly lived was when the helicopter would fly them to shock trauma, and the way you would know if they were dead was when the body was covered with a white sheet and the ambulance would haul them up out of there.

Big-H got locked up for attempted murder when I was about 9 yrs old. The only way I knew it was him was because another nigga hollered out his name in the yard. I pulled him up later on that day and let him know who I was. He remembered my mother, aunts, uncles, and my grandparents.

About a couple of weeks later we started working out together, he had me on a serious work out. Monday-Friday, 8-10am we was outside lifting weights. [I was about 140 lbs bench pressing 275. Big-H had me strong as shit, while I was up Jessup.]

About 3-4 times out of the week, he would have C.O's bring us sub sandwiches, shrimp, even fried chicken from off of the street. My last year and ½ in prison went fast. I did about 3 ½ years on my 5 year sentence because of good time.

The whole time I was in denial, it wasn't a day that went past that I didn't think about money. The only thing that's worse than wasted time is time wasted. Money and me were like co-defendants, we were always going to be together. While I was incarcerated, between making sure my mother was living ok and lawyer fees, I was going home broke. I learned that having money meant I needed for nothing, but having none means needing it more.

My release date was September 12th, I couldn't wait to get home. The day that I was scheduled to leave, I was awakened early that morning by loud talking in the dorm. When I lifted my head up from under the covers, I witnessed niggas crowded around the two T.V's, stuck like deer's in front of head lights. After brushing my teeth, I walked towards the T.V and got to a spot next to Ron.

I said, "What happened yo?"

Ron said, "The terrorist is hijacking our airplanes and using them to attack on U.S soil".

From the look of the building burning on the television I knew that he wasn't lying.

I said, "Damn, that nigga Ben Laden said, "if Bush became President that the American people would pay dearly".

The facility locked us in our dorms that whole day for safety reasons because Jessup was only a ½ hour from B.W.I airport. I wasn't worried that the terrorist attack would interfere with me going home the next day because if the computers just so happened to go down, I had my commitment papers to show proof of my release date.

The facility had me packed up about 8 o'clock that next morning. I gave Ron my information and told him to call me when he got out. Big-H walked me to the gate. A van waited to transfer me to BrockBridge. After Big-H gave me a fatherly hug he told me he'll see me in about a year.

When I walked out of Brockbridge gates it was about 10:30 am, Black was smiling sitting on his car. The expression on his face showed that he was proud to see his little brother survived the concrete jungle once again. It was the same look he had been getting use to. I would've bet anybody that I wouldn't be stacking letters, and that I would be stacking money forever.

The only thing that I realized when I was doing my bid was that the only people that will stick by you is your family. In most cases they don't even stick around because you can't spell "families" with out the "lies. My mother, brother, Meka, Monique and Sherica held me down my whole bid. My father even came to see me after he did his 18 months for violation of his probation.[The females went with the money and the niggas just ain't shit. They bring you flowers when your dead, but no soup when your sick.]

When you know that one of your men is locked up, it's real disrespectful to ask his girl or family members "is he alright or does he need anything". Now, you know that a nigga is locked-up so that person ain't making the money he use to. Why would you ask if he need something, that shouldn't even be a question. Niggas!!

Chapter 24

Present

"H.H . . . . wake up yo, they opening the doors!"
After putting my shoes on and grabbing my chair. I followed with the crowed of inmates towards the phones.

After about a half hour, I finally got on and called over to my grandparents house. She told me that my mother waited around until about 10 o'clock this morning for me to call. I informed her that somebody got killed in the jail this morning, so they kept us on lockdown. I don't know why I told her that because I knew she and my mother were going to worry themselves to death about me. My grandmother kept me on the phone the whole 15 minutes, before hanging up. She sent me her love and prayers as usual. I told her I would call back about 5 o'clock pm to talk to my mother.

On the T.V, inmates were watching guiding light, so I sat my chair down and acted like I was interested in the stories. I couldn't believe that I was in this situation, the F.E.D.s didn't have any evidence on me, just niggas running off with their mouths. The "Boca-Raton" huh.

A couple of minutes later, my cousin pulled his chair up then said,

"yo, they say we was on the news and in the newspapers".

With a discussed look on my face I said,

"the reason why we was getting this publicity is because the police got shot".

He looked at me with a dumb look on his face then said,

"yeah . . . I know."

"Fed-Up!"

The C.O yelled, Lunch!!! It wasn't nothing to look forward to because I knew it was some bullshit. The veil patty was hard and looked like fried liver. I gave that shit to -H but I ate the cookies and drank the milk. He tapped me on the shoulder and said,

"yo, somebody want you at the door".

I thought to myself, "who the fuck know me up here".

I walked to the door to see that it was my man "Cliff".

[Cliff was an O.G. from a project in Naptown called "Intown", but everybody knew it as "4th ward".

I said, "what's up my nigga?"

He said, "ain't shit young blood, how you holding up?"

I said, "I'm good . . . you know this just another part of the game."

Cliff told me that he was currently locked up over B.C.C.C and he comes over to the Supermax Monday-Friday to clean the hallways. He also informed me that some niggas from down Robinwood let him know that I was over in the max.

I said, "Damn . . . word travel fast".

Cliff said, "They say they gonna send you some tobacco over tomorrow so you can buy some food to hold you until commissary day".

I said, "tell them niggas that I appreciate that because its dry week and I can't go to the store until next week".

Cliff said, "keep your head up and I'll see you tomorrow".

We both gave each other a pound at the door before walking off. I got back to my chair and told -H about the tobacco that was coming tomorrow.

After The Guiding light went off, I told -H that I was going back to the cell to lay back once the doors open back up. I still needed time so that this F.E.D shit could settle in my brain, I still was in somewhat of a shock. He told me that he was going to chill and jump back on the phone before count time.

About 10 minutes later, the C.O. came in and yelled,

"Doors open!"

After grabbing my chair, I walked to my cell. After the doors closed, I laid on my bunk and started to reminisce about the past.

Chapter 25

Product of My Environment

Black took me to the Annapolis Mall and bought me a couple pair of shoes and some clothes, then we headed over to our grandparents house out Bestgate.

While riding up the drive way, I looked around and noticed that the area still looked the same. My whole family greeted me with open arms. They told me how good I looked and that they couldn't believe how long my hair was. My dreads came down to my shoulders and the tank top showed off the muscles that was the product of me lifting weights while I was in prison. I wasn't a pretty nigga, but I also wasn't to bad on the eyes either.

My cousins were no longer little anymore, they looked like grown men. From the stories my brother told me while I was gone, these niggas been off the hook lately. Annapoliteans labeled us as the "hyenas", because anybody who knew my family would say that we had an ill laugh that sounded exactly like the animal. The laugh got handed down in our family from generation to generation. If we were ready to beef with anybody, we would come together in a pack. Not to say that we couldn't handle ourselves, but in most cases that's just how it was.

My mother pulled me to the side and handed me a $100 and with a smile on her face, she told me not to spend it all in one place. I told myself, "that was going be the last time that I ever accepted my mothers hard earned money."

A couple of hours passed, and after stuffing myself with the home cooked meal my family made, black and I headed over to Eastport with the hyenas following suit.

Eastport looked trashier, and smaller, but to me it was still home sweet home. That wasn't important though, the only thing that I was thinking about was finding Cheek-O so that I could get some of that good cocaine I was hearing he was getting. Black informed me that the Drug game been fucked up since the Terrorist attack and that since it's around Election time that just made it worse.

Cheek-O was supposed to have been the only one that was going up to Yankeeville (N.Y.) buying weight. Early that year the F.E.D.s had locked up Vince and Bell. Skip was doing 10 yrs up Jessup over "the cut", Jay was doing 10 yrs on the farm. Glass and Chopper were all buying from fluid who was Cheek-O's older brother, Chuck moved to Ohio and Honk called it quits and moved to V.A.

When everybody saw me, they greeted me and acted like they were glad to see me. After walking around a little while longer, I finally found Cheek-O over Harbor House in front of the 1165 building.

Cheek-O and about 10 Eastporterricans greeted me and showed the proper respect.

I said, "Cheek-O, let me holler at you for a minute?"

We walked around the corner into the gap.

I said, "yo, you know I'm hungry and I know you going to look out for me?"

He said, "I got you shorty, just take some time for a little while and observe Eastport, because a lot of shit has changed since you been gone".

I said, "I'm fucked up right now yo, I need to start eaten again".

Cheek-O looked at me and must've saw how serious I was. He pulled out an 8-Ball from his pocket then said,

"bring me back $100 . . . you know prices is sky high, the regular price is $175". I reached in my pocket and gave him the $100 my mother gave me.

He said, "after you sell that, come holler back at me with all the money you've made".

Cheek-O gave me a brotherly hug and ensured me that he was gonna look out for me until I got back on my feet.

Later that day I ran into Sherica, she stayed in touch and even came to see me while I was up Jessup. Her once skinny body had now blossomed into a sexy butterfly. Sherica looked like Megan Good with some nice size breast. She gave me a hug and a kiss on the cheek then said,

"why didn't you tell me that you was coming home today?"

I said, "I didn't know because after the terrorist attack, the prison was saying that nobody would be released until after that situation". I lied.

She smiled then said,

"yeah right".

I gave out a Hyena laugh.

✱ [She said, "I finally received my R.N (Registered Nurse) license and I'm going back to school in December to enhance my career . . . and I just got my own place down Newtown-20 and if you want to, you can come visit me later on".

I said, "if I got time, I'll call you later on tonight". After giving me another hug and kiss she said,

"hopefully I'll see you later".

I smiled then said,

"we'll see".

I wasn't worried about any pussy right now, I was on a paper chase. One of the rules to the Drug game was, "once you get your money right the females going to come". Being with a female wasn't really important to me at that moment. Besides, as soon as word got around that I was home, the project bitches came left and right. Sherica wasn't your average project chick though. Yeah, she lived in The Housing Authority but she was trying to better herself by going to school so that she could get the fuck out.

I stayed outside until the next morning, I had refused to go in the house for the night without getting rid of the work that I had. It was about 8 o'clock am when I finally went down to Allen's apartment, to my mother's boyfriends place to get some rest. Before going to sleep, I counted my money and to my surprise I had $430. After I sold the first 8-ball, I made $250. I went right back and bought another 8-ball from Cheek-O. I figured I'll give him a call about 1 p.m. to buy some more work.

When I woke up my mother had some breakfast on the kitchen table for me with a note that red,

✱ "I'm going to get my hair done out "Lisa's Solon, don't forget to go and see your probation officer . . .Love Ya!

I got in touch with Cheek-O at about 1:30p.m. and told him that I got $400 and I'd be over the way around 3p.m.

I took a shower, got myself together and went around to the court house to see my P.O., Mr. Zelco, who was court appointed to my case. He was a fat over weighted pig with glasses. He looked like a young version of "Boss Hog" off of the Dukes a Hazard. The first thing he ask me was,

"are you any kin to the Walders down Lothian Maryland?"

I said, "yeah".

With a discussed look on his face he said,

"I hope that you're nothing like them . . . because if you are, your ass would be back up Jessup before you know it". He then informed me that I would be reporting to him every 5th day of the month, and that he would be taking a urine sample. When he dismissed me I looked at him and smiled while walking out his office.

I got over to Eastport a little after 3 o'clock that afternoon and found Cheek-O in his usual spot in front of the 1165 building. After he greeted me he said,

"follow me into the building".

In the building I gave him $400 then said,

"I been grinding all night long".

Cheek-O reached in his pocket gave me a half ounce then said,

"yo, they go for $600, but don't worry about the rest of the money".

I said, "good looking out".

I grinded that whole day, I was trying to get that money and fast.

I ran into Sherica about 7 o'clock that night.

She said, "you must've been real busy last night?"

I smiled then said, "yeah, I was out here trying to make a couple of dollars".

She said, "yeah right".

I said, "what you doing tonight?"

She said, "waiting on you to call me".

I thought to myself that I should treat myself because I damn sure earned it, plus Sherica was looking good.

I told her, "I'll be down -20 about 11 o'clock.

She said, "don't have me waiting up for nothing". After smiling she walked off.

I caught a cab down -20 about 11:30 p.m. Niggas was outside everywhere. Newtown -20 was another project in Naptown that was a deathtrap, one way in and one way out. These niggas down here wouldn't hesitate for a second to put a bullet in your head and keep it moving. I was good though because niggas knew who I was and with my name came a reputation.

I ran into two O.G niggas, Dirty Nose and Pops. After we greeted each other with the proper respect and a little conversation, I kept it moving to Sherica's building.

I knocked on the door and Sherica opened it up with just a bath towel on.

She said, "you late".

I said, "I got caught in traffic".

She smiled then said,

"you lying".

I gave out a hyena laugh then walked into her apartment. Sherica wasted no time to show me how much she missed me. She pushed me on the couch and started stripping me naked like she was robbing me of my clothes. My dick didn't waste any time to show off his length.

Sherica stood up and unleashed the towel she had on so that she could show me how big her breast got. She smiled, then she looked into my eyes and stuck her tongue out, then slowly started to lick her lips. My dick head beat like it had a severe headache, it felt like it was trying to bust out of its skin. She took her right hand and tried to rap it around my four inch wide anaconda as best as she could, then she started to message it up and down. It felt so good that I had to lean back, my eyes just rolled in the back of my head. I tried to think about something else besides Sherica going to work on me because I was about to cum at any moment,

With her soft voice she said,

"does that feel good?"

With a stuttering low voice I said,

"he-hell, ye-yeah".

She let out a little chuckle. The couple of minutes while she messaged my dick, I was on cloud nine, but what quickly bought me back to reality was when she started sucking on my balls.

"Oh-Shit! I hollered out loud.

I couldn't hold it back anymore, the message while sucking my balls at the same time made me unleash something terrible. The ejaculation seemed like it would never end. The cum made a squishy sound on my dick as Sherica continued to do what she started. I was paralyzed, I'm thinking I'm having a stroke. I grabbed her hand and pushed it away then said,

"Ho-Hold-Up!"

She smiled as if she was satisfied at the way she was making me feel, then said,

"What?"

I said, "I need a little break".

Sherica looked at my 9" long and 4" wide Anaconda standing tall then said,

"that's not what I see".

She jumped on top of me and guided my snake into her hot soaking wet pussy, then she carefully eased up and down until she couldn't take anymore. I came again immediately. By her biting her lip and the hot fluids running down her legs, I knew she was enjoying herself. Her moaning and the multiple orgasms she was having made it official that I was handling my business. Every time I tried to pull her hips down so that she could feel me up in her rib cage, she would dig her finger nails into my back harder and harder. By her acting like that, it was letting me know that she wasn't ready for the best of me yet.

Sherica road my dick for about a ½ hour none stop, her big ass breast flapped up and down, up against her stomach as if they were boxing each other.

After the third time I came, I went out like a light. The way Sherica was shaking you would've thought that she was having a seizure. She laid her helpless body on mine like we were Siamese twins.

That was the first pussy I had since I came home from up Jessup. The three and a half years while I was incarcerated made me excited, and anxious about the feeling of a female, but more importantly, I knew that it's always business before pleasure.

When I woke up, my ass was sticky, and soaking wet from us having sex on the black leather couch.

Sherica was gone, but it was a note on the living room table that red,

"I didn't want to wake you but I had to go to work, call me later".

When I looked at the clock it was 12:30 p.m. I reached in my pocket and pulled out the $565 and the quarter ounce of coke I had left. I said to myself, "time to go to work".

I got my sister to come and pick me up and take me down the country so that I could holler at my cousin -C. He still had shit on lockdown and he still had our little cousins holding shit down for him when he wasn't there.

-C gave me an ounce of some alright Cocaine and told me to holler back at him whenever I can.

After seeing my grandmother and the rest of my family, I went to see Monique.

I've learned to respect the fact that she had a little boyfriend but I knew that I'd always have a special place in her heart. So that she could be discrete about the situation, she met me down at Dash-in. When she jumped out of her x5 BMW truck, just by looking at her got my dick hard instantly.

Monique greeted me with the same tight hug and pretty smile that she always did when she visited me up Jessup.

I said, "What's up?"

While pressing her thigh up against my dick she said,

"hey baby . . . when did you come home?"

I said, "this morning".

While smiling, she said, "you lying".

I gave out the Hyena laugh then said,

"how is your boyfriend doing?"

She said, "C-mon Booh, lets not go there . . . you know that you'll always have a special place in my heart".

I said, "yeah, I know".

We sat in her truck and talked for a little while, reminiscing about back in the day. Monique informed me that she had received her Realtors license and that she was currently working for a private company that helped people find shelter after disasters had struck their homes.

Monique said, "when I get some free time from my job and my relationship, we'll spend some personal time together".

I agreed.

Before leaving, she leaned over and gave me a tongue kiss while squeezing my dick then said,

"don't be a stranger now that your home".

I said, "you don't have to worry about that . . . just make sure you call me for that quality time".

She smiled then said,

"Boy, you know I got you".

By the time November came, I had about $10,000 in my stash.

Black and about seven of the Hyenas took me up to Baltimore to the strip clubs for my birthday, Baltimore street was so packed that the police had to block off certain parts, so that nobody could drive through.

We had to park down the street in the parking lot across from the Cheese Cake Factory.

Little -D said, "pop the trunk Black so that I can put the chopper in it".

Little -D was always prepared for war, but he also had a short temper, as did the other hyenas that rolled with us.

After popping the trunk, Black said,

"I'm keeping the D.E. on me just incase niggas up here start acting up".

✱ While I was up Jessup, Black informed me that him and about six East Puerto-Ricans got robbed in the parking garage across the street from the strip club. That spot was a death trap for niggas on club nights.

The first club we hit was "Foxy Ladies", we paid to get in and had to buy drinks. The bitches in Foxy Ladies was beat the fuck up, the bullet holes and stretch marks only added to the disappointment. The smell of ass and funky pussy had me feeling like I had to throw up.

After staying for about 20 minutes, we went next door to "Norma Jeans". Norma Jeans was in a class of its own. All the females in there were sexy as shit, plus their bodies were in shape. They were so pretty it made you wanna ask them why were they even stripping. You had to be on point though, because if you wasn't careful, you could easily get tricked by one of those bitches. "Got's to B-more careful"!!!

After spending an hour and a couple hundred dollars in Norma's, we went to Stage Door. We decided to by pass the Larry Flint strip club though because you couldn't touch them bitches anyway.

Stage Door was a hole in the wall, some what similar to Foxy Ladies. After staying for about 15 minutes, we got the fuck up out of there also.

When I got back down to Allen's Apartment I had to take a shower because I smelled like strippers from all the lap dances I was getting treated to. The white T-shirt I had on got thrown in the trash because I knew that the stains of funk and bootie juices wasn't coming out.

By the time New Years came, I was buying a brick of my own. I felt like I was on top of the world. At that day and time, "I was back up on my feet like insoles".

Cheek-O saw how fast I was coming up in the game, so he started charging me regular prices. Yeah, I started looking at him differently, but I bit my tongue because he still was one of the only hustlers over Eastport that was getting good cocaine at the time.

I promised myself that when I get back on top, I was going to make niggas pay.

The flunky looked at his roll model who was also his Boss and said,

"you been working these streets for about forty years now . . . so why haven't you retired yet?"

Bossman said, "years ago in Novemeber I had plans to retire . . . after being on the force for 25 years . . . I got a phone call and was told that my daughter just over dosed off of crack cocaine. When I got to the hospital, the doctors told me that she didn't make it".

The flunky said, "damn, I'm sorry to here that".

Bossman said, "I lost my wife a year before that because a crack head shot her in the head before carjacking her . . . now that I've lost my only child to crack at the age of sixteen, I have nothing left to do in my life."

The Flunky looked at his partner and saw a tear drop from his eye. This was the first time he had ever seen his Boss show this side of himself. It was an emotional moment.

The flunky said, "I'm sorry to hear that".

Bossman said, "I never found out who the nigger was that sold her the drugs, so I decided to stay on the force and make sure that every crack dealer felt the pain that I've felt. I joined the Academy fresh out of high school. I just turned 58 years old last month, what the hell am I going to do if I retire. I'm satisfied, retirement to me is like a "Death sentence with benefits".

The flunky said, "did you ever think about becoming a detective?"

Bossman said, "it crossed my mind in my younger days, I've learned to love being in the field 24/7.

Bossman pulled up next to his informant at the back of Eastport shopping center.

Larry was once a Big time Drug dealer in Naptown in his early days, until he broke one of the most important rules of the streets, he started getting high off of his own supply. Now, the neighborhood super stars paid him no homage and disrespected him every chance they got. Ashy Larry, was what he was called throughout the projects because he smoked so much crack that his skin was dried up like a prune. Larry figured, since the young hustlers won't pay him for making the way, he rather snitch on them to teach them a lesson. Bossman rolled down the window and said,

"what you got for me tonight?"

With his powdered lips, ashy Larry said,

"man, little Booh is coming up fast in the game".

The flunky said, "who he getting his weight from?"

Ashy Larry said, "Cheek-O, who else".

Bossman said, "you think I'm going to keep on paying you to support your crack habit while you keep given us information we already know?"

Ashy Larry said, "all my information I give y'all is official".

The flunky said, "you told us that little Booh killed white boy Mike back in the day, but we couldn't get enough evidence to charge him".

Ashy Larry said, "he did kill white boy Mike . . . little Booh just to smart to ever get caught, he's not like these average Hustlers out here".

Bossman said, "that little motherfucker ain't that smart. I tell you what, "make it your business to find out everything you can about what he's doing".

Ashy Larry said, "what about Cheek-O?"

Bossman said, "don't worry about Cheek-O no more, because his days are numbered in low digits and he don't even no it yet".

After Bossman gave Ashy Larry a $20 dollar bill, and his famous joker smile, he pulled off.

Chapter   26

The Connect

For Valentines Day, I decided to treat myself to a trip. Sherica and I went to Jamaica, I deserved it, plus Sherica had proven to be helpful to me in many situations.

I used two I.D.'s. and my Birth Certificate because I didn't have a passport.

That was the first time I had ever gotten onto an airplane. The first class seat didn't comfort me much because the bumps and shakes from the turbulence gave us the same ride as the people in coach. From the air, I could see that the water in Jamaica was three different colors, it looked like paradise.

Montego Bay was beautiful, even though Jamaica was a poor country, it was a pretty place.

We left B.W.I at 42degrees, and arrived in the Islands which was 85 degrees. When we landed and we walked outside the airport, you could smell the hot tropical air.

When we got into the station, it seemed like everybody was trying to sell us weed. The people who worked there were practically on there hands and knees for us. The Jamaicans were so use to seeing white people visit the island, so to them it was somewhat strange when they saw a black couple. They knew that we had money. If I was in their shoes, I could see that also because a U.S. dollar was worth $56 in Jamaica.

Everybody from the island called me "Rasta Man" because of my dreadlocks which hung down to my shoulders.

After checking in, getting our luggage, and tipping about 10 Jamaican workers, it was about a 40 minute ride to the four star hotel.

The whole van ride Shenica and I was tripping on how we were riding on the wrong side of the road. Jamaicans were selling fish, eel, and crabs, while goats were running around everywhere.

During the journey to the hotel, we witnessed the poverty that was on the beautiful island. The small shacks that the majority of the population lived in, looked and was the same size of regular sheds. We also witnessed the Big houses on the top of the hills. The driver informed us that the people who had a lot of money lived there, mainly drug dealers.

When we got to the Sandals Resort, the hotel was big as shit. Everybody who worked at the hotel treated us like a King and Queen. After checking in, the hotel staff supervisor named "Leidy", gave us a credit card with our names on it and informed us that while we were at the Resort that all of our food and drinks were free as long as we had our cards on us. I bought a couple of thousand on me anyway just in case we wanted to take some memories back to the states with us. After a couple of minutes, she escorted us to our room.

She was a sexy chocolate Jamaican with a phat ass. Leidy was about 5 ft tall and looked like Naomi Cambell. Her Jamaican accent just put the icing on the cake.

I said, "where you from down here Leidy?"

She said, "I'm from Kingston, but I came to Montego Bay to work".

I said, "were trying to go to Kingston before we leave the island. I didn't come to Jamaica to stay at the resort, I want to see the real Jamaica".

Leidy looked at me with her sexy brown eyes and said,

"be careful".

I knew that Kingston was a jungle from the stories I heard back home and reading the air Jamaica newspaper on the plane, I knew it was dangerous to be walking around down there. I ain't stupid, I just was planning on getting somebody to drive us through there so we could get a first hand look at the so called "jungle".

When we got to our room, Leidy informed us that our bags would be here shortly. I gave her a twenty dollar bill for her service. After taking the money, Leidy gave me her sexy smile and then said,

"if you all need anything, call to the front desk and ask for me".

The room was like a Presidential suite, and to top that off, the view was out of this world. When we walked out on the balcony, we could see the whole Montego Bay. The look on Sherica's face showed that she was happy to be there.

Later on that night, we decided not to order room service. We went out to eat down by the beach. When we got to the Japanese restaurant, they seated us at a table with another couple. By the way they were talking, I could tell that they were Hungarian. They greeted us, as we did them. Blonco looked like "Uncle J.R." off of the T.V. series "The Sopranos" and Toray looked like a model. With her blond hair, she easily could've been mistaken for the model "Coco", Ice T's wife, without the body.

We got along just fine. That was the first time that I sat in a restaurant while my food was being cooked right in front of me. The chef did all types of tricks with the food and the knives. Our eyes were wide open the whole time. After he finished, with his Jamaican accent he said,

"don't try any of that at home".

Everybody at the table laughed. While we were eating, Blonco looked at me and said,

"Where y'all from?"

I said, "Maryland".

He said, "I got a cousin that lives near Baltimore".

I said, "we live near Baltimore too".

After about an hour of eating and conversation with each other, they invited us to the bar by the beach to have a couple of drinks, we accepted. At the bar, while Sherica and Toray talked and admired each others clothes, Blonco asked me to take a walk with him. While walking along the beach, Blonco said to me,

"are you in the business?"

With a serious look on my face I said,

"What kind of business?"

He said, "what do you know about cocaine?"

I didn't know him before that day.

I said, "what you police?"

He laughed then said, "no, but that's a smart answer to give to somebody who you just met".

In his eyes I saw no lies, so I said,

"I know enough".

He said, "can you handle 40 kilos a month?"

I said, "hell yeah!"

I gave Blonco the exact location where I was at and told him that I only had about $48,000 to my name. He asured me that he could send 40 kilos of pure cocaine every 1st of the month and that he would give me the kilos for $25,000 a piece. He informed me not to worry about the first package of money, just bring it back when the next time I re-up.

That was good money, because I was giving Cheek-O $32,000 for a kilo. Plus an extra $500 to the mule for bringing that shit back from up Yankeeville. More importantly, I didn't have to put any money up.

Blonco explained that since the terrorist attack that its been harder to bring cocaine to America, but as soon as everything gets back to normal that the prices would go back down.

Things were starting to finally go my way. Soon I'd be getting some good coke for a low price, and I'm getting it right at my doorstep.

Blonco gave me a number and told me to call it when I get back home. So that he would be sure to put the order in for me.

The next couple of days in Jamaica, I was on cloud nine. Shenica and I didn't get to go to Kingston because nobody wanted to drive us down there. They all said that it was too dangerous. Kingston must be a complete jungle for real because they were from the island and they were scared to go down there. I wasn't mad though, because we still had a good time, and more importantly, I ran into a "Major Connect".

This couldn't have happened to me at a better time in my life. The way Cheek-O was charging me for a brick, it was time for me to "stop being a waiter and start getting a meal myself".

[As soon as I got back to Naptown, I called Blonco and he assured me a white boat with a huge blue crab on both sides would be at the Annapolis Harbor at 12 noon on the first of the month.]

C h a p t e r   2 7

Annapolis Harbor

Downtown Annapolis is a Historic spot. People from the Naval Academy, tourist and Annapoliteans enjoyed the scenery that the harbor showed.

✱⌉The "boat shows" that came to the Capital of Maryland each year was like hitting the lottery for the underworld of Naptown. The only time that I would visit was when I went to eat at Buddy's Crabs for breakfast.

The crack heads terrorized the area by robbing, stealing and assaulting any and everyone they could. The prostitutes sold their bodies to the Politicians and Naval Academy soldiers, while the drug dealers would sell their product to any and everybody who wanted to get high.

I called a meeting for the family to drop down the law. I had to make sure that we were all on the same page "Loyalty before Royalty". The art of a good business is a good middle man, because he got to put together the foot soldiers. At the meeting was my brother Black,-C, Vedo, little-D, Pooh, little-One, Fat Boy, T-Bone, Muse, Damion and Waun. All of us made up part of the "family", and more importantly, we were all blood related. The first thing I did was give each of them a beeper number because I never used cell phones for business, that was dangerous. With the number, I gave each one of them a code, so when they beeped me I knew who it was.

I told -C, since he was already running this down the country I wanted him to continue to do so.

I told Vedo, since he was up P.G. County on M.L.K (Martin Luther King) doing his thing to continue to do so as well.

Damion was back and forth up Baltimore, so immediately he was going to set up shop, so the family could get some of that Baltimore love.

For the rest of the family, I had a master plan. I told Pooh to go down "Woodz", Fat boy to go out "Gardens", Waun to go to "4th Ward", T-Bone to go down "Newtown-20" and I sent Little-D down "Bywaters".

Muse never did get involved with the drug game, so I put him in charge of being the enforcer. Whenever the family ran across a problem with somebody, it was his job to send them Hyenas in to cause chaos. I sent Muse to go buy some Alphebets (A.K's, A.R-15, D.E's, etc . . .) and some numbers (45's, 38's, 9's, 50-cal. Etc . . .).

I told the family, instead of going to the projects and strong arming their way to the cash, pick out an individual who meets the standard requirements for getting money then give them a shot of the "American dream". If niggas can't come to some type of agreement with y'all, I'll get Muse to send them Hyenas down there and burn the block up. "Fuck it", if we couldn't get no money down there, than they won't either. We all let out the Hyena laugh, but this time the laugh was more deadlier. We all been starving for so long, and now it was time to eat. Just like a pack of wild hyenas, we were going to eat everything. The plan was when we get done with the Capital of Maryland, there was going to be nothing left.

Little-One was the baby out of the pack with a lion heart, who wasn't corrupted by the politics of the game. The 12 year old was my protégé. I loved him like a son and he looked up to me like a father figure. I informed him that he was going to stay with me and operate over Eastport, so that I can keep an eye on him.

I bought five walkie talkies, one for me, one for the little-one and the other three for my workers. The crack heads were posted up over Eastport like stop signs, it was impossible for the police to approach the project without me knowing. I had the whole 1100 block tight like a womb and no room for intruders. To add icing on the cake, I had a scanner to give me heads up just in case one of the fiends decided to leave their post to go get high. If this was to ever happen the punishment was brutal.

The next day I was down at the Annapolis Harbor at 11a.m. sharp. I went to Buddy's Crabs and got a booth close to the window so that I could see when the boats came in.

After eating off of the buffet line, the boat that I was looking for came in a little after 12 noon. I couldn't explain the feeling that I felt, a warm rush came over my body. It was some what like waiting for an A.I.D's test result that after a couple of weeks had finally come back "negative".

After taking a deep breath I said to myself "Damn, Blonco came through".

After the boat took about 15 minutes to park, I walked down to the pier hoping to pick my package up. When I got to the boat I recognized that two little white kids and a woman who looked as though she was their mother, walked off. In a low voice I said, "What the fuck". When they walked passed me, they never looked my way. The closer I got to the boat, the slower I walked. The way I saw it, my hopes and dreams were relying on this package. Before I knew it, a Hungarian voice yelled out, "Excuse me!", I stopped and saw a grey haired man stick his head out of the boat. I stopped and said nothing, all I did was stare.

He said, "could you come and help me with my bags?" At the time I was already upset because I was starting to think that Blonco was full of shit.

I said, "help you with your bags, what I look like a slave to you?"

While giving me eye contact, he took his pointer finger and signaled me to come inside the boat. When I became sane again from my rage, it came to me that this person had the same voice as Blonco, there was still some hope that this was my package.

I was real cautious going on the boat because I still didn't know what to expect. When I walked inside, the grey haired man was sitting on a couch. He extended his hand and said,

"I'm Diablo."

Diablo smiled at me while pointing at a big black gym bag beside him.

He said, "Blonco sends his regards".

I sat there for a couple of seconds looking at the black bag like I was star struck. I thought to myself, "this is it . . . I'm going to run this city with an iron fist".

Diablo said, "I'll see you next month, same time same place".

I said, "I'll have your money next time I see you".

While smiling Diablo said, "yes".

The bag was heavy as shit. In it was 40 Kilos, each weighting 2.2 pounds a piece. I walked off of the boat with the cocaine with no problem, flagged a cab down and headed over to Eastport for the road to success.

C h a p t e r   2 8

"Paid in Full"

A month had passed, I took Diablo the money I owed from the first package and just like Blonco promised me the package always came on the first of the month] They say that in this profession the more money you start to make, the more problems you start to get.

The only problem I had was counting and separating the money. That was the first time that I ever got a good look at a million dollars. That shit looked beautiful. I couldn't wait to have my own stashed away. I didn't trust a money machine, so I had to count everything out by hand. I was like that little white boy on the Bruce Willis movie, "the sixth sense". "I see Dead people!" I was talking about Benjamin Franklin and all them other dead president's on the bills though. I used to get headaches so bad from counting for so long that I would black out, when I would wake up the money just be staring at me in my face.

I had to put all the $100 bills in $50,000 stacks, all the $50 bills in $20,000 stacks, all the $20 bills in $10,000 stacks and all the $10 bills in $5,000 stacks. I never sent $1 bills because it took-up to much space, so I just spent the Washington's on the little project kids who had no hope for the future at all. To them it wasn't realistic that they were going to make it up out of the hood, and I had the feeling that they were right.

My finger tips would be so black from counting so much money that I had to scrub them with soap and bleach.

When I first started messing with the drug game, I was "engaged" to the cash. Since then, I've upgraded. Now I was "married" to the money and kilos of cocaine was my best man. The money promised to love me through sickness and good health. I do too, until death do us part. I took these vowels very seriously.

Hustlers from over Eastport were buying from me except for Cheek-O and a couple other Super stars. I guess their pride wouldn't let them buy some bricks for low prices from a person who had only been home six months. It wasn't my fault that they were stuck on stupid, I had to keep it moving. Why wouldn't you want to buy some weight from somebody who is bringing it to you right at your door step. I wasn't worried about it though, because if I did have any extra kilos left over from the package it wouldn't be any problem getting rid of them.

Almost every project in Naptown cooperated with my request, they either bought directly or indirectly from me. The only Hustlers that wasn't going for it was down "Bywaters". This wasn't any surprise to me because these niggas had a couple of super stars who were also selling some weight. In a situation like this, only two things had to happen. I had to find where their main source was and get rid of them or interfere with their cash flow. That way niggas down Bywaters wouldn't have any choice but to buy from me. Where I'm from niggas call it "Gorilla pimping". It is what it is though. I got Muse to send them hyenas down there to burn the block up. Fuck it, if the family couldn't get any money down there then they wasn't either, then we would see who was going to take the loss. Them Bywater niggas wasn't no whores either, they came back at the family just as strong.

I ran into Bossman and his flunky on Sanky's street the next day.

With the joker smile Bossman said,

"welcome home little Booh".

The grey that showed on his head and face let me know that he was getting to old to try to keep up with me now.

The flunky said, "we missed you".

I said, "your mother said the same thing".

I continued to walk past Sanky's and went in the direction of the shopping center because I knew that I was still band from the Housing Authority Property.

While driving slow beside me, Bossman said,

"I heard y'all got a little war going on with them Bywater niggers?"

I said, "I don't know what you talking bout".

He said, "you ain't got to worry about us interfering . . . I would rather for you niggers kill each other off . . ."

After giving out a laugh, the flunky pulled off.

The war went on for about a year. I didn't give a fuck though because my money was still coming in. There was beef when we saw each other at the American Legion, Elkes, Peelers Club and even at the mall. Anywhere at any time we bumped heads there was drama. The Alphabet's and Numbers ranged out all hours of the day and night. A.P.D (Annapolis Police Department) got word of the beef, so they set patrol cars up on each block to try and stop the violent acts.

My little cousin -D got locked up in the process for attempted murder because a nigga down Bywater I.D'ed him as being the one who shot him in the ass during a recent drive by.

Reality set in, I wasn't going to risk my operation and let one of these niggas tell on me about a body.

"I rather let the dollar bill rain on me instead of letting one of these niggas make a name off me". Niggas know the code of the street, if somebody get slumped, they just get slumped.

I sent word down Bywaters to tell them that I'll call a truce if the nigga who told on little -D don't go to court, and for his pain and suffering I'll give him $10,000, Five up front and Five after the court date. They agreed and the beef was over.

I paid O'Neel $8,000 to take the case, little -D was home in a month. The prosecutor had to drop the charges because they didn't have a witness anymore. Little-D informed me that his cousin on his fathers side name "Little Mike" was hanging down Bywaters and was trying to jump on our team. I told him to call his cousin up and take him some work down there, Royal and Copeland street was going to add the icing on the cake to my operation.

Money was coming in fast and I loved it, I was getting the best cocaine in the Capital of Maryland, and I had a bunch of hungry niggas that was behind me 100%.

The kilos of cocaine that I was getting from Blonco was pure, just like a cup of Virgins blood. I had to use a razor blade to cut through the duct tape, then through the rubber, and then through the plastic. The stars that were getting money in Naptown called it "safe sex". The stamp on the kilos made them official and would let you know what family over Columbia/Mexico they came from. Every time I would cook a kilo up I would gain a quarter brick, and it would still be good.

Any Hustler who ever bought weight from up Yankeeville (N.Y.) would tell you that 9-times out of 10, Poppy don't like to sell you kilo's still packaged up the way they get it. Poppy would rather take out from each kilo, use a compressed machine to add some cut to it, then sell it to you like that. To keep it real, that is being smart though, because if the cocaine was good and it can hold the cut, that's more money in their pocket. Now that I was getting kilos the same way Poppy was getting'em, I decided to use that same technique to help me continue to rape the drug game in Naptown.

I charged the family $30,000 a brick, and the outsiders would get them for $31,500. Since Cheek-O was selling his kilos for $32,000 a piece, I figured I would charge less so I could take his clients from him. Don't let it be around election time (November) either, because I got my "Buy any means on" or whenever there was a "drought". In Corporate America it's called "price gauging". My connect kept his word and my package was sent to me every month. When I asked him about the drought he said, "no such thing".

Out of the 40 kilos I got a month, I only wholesaled about 10. The other 30, what I didn't give to the family on consignment, I whipped (cooked) up. The 9 ounces that I would gain off of every cook up, I would sell for $7,500 a piece, add that to the $5,000 I was getting off of each wholesaled kilo, you do the math on how much money I was making off of a package. I was always singing "Happy Birthday" because I was getting that "Super Cake". My money stash had gotten so big that I had to burry it in the woods so I wouldn't have to worry about A.P.D. or the D.E.s taking it.

I was treating the Capital of Maryland like a big game of "Monopoly". The family was part owner of every project in Naptown, so if any money came on the properties we wanted in on it.

That spring without either one of us knowing, Cheek-O and I bought a whip (vehicle) from different spots. I bought an S.T.S. Cadillac and he bought a Cadillac truck. I paid cash for mine, and so did he. Even though we were in competition with one another, Cheek-O and I always gave each other the proper respect. "Honor amongst Hustlers".

Chapter 29

Reality

My sister "Meeka" was still throwing parties as she started doing when I was paying my debt to society up Jessup.

Meeka was doing good in life, she got a government job, got her own house, and more importantly she needed "no man". She was independent and her girlfriends who she hung with were also. From a niggas point of view, Meeka was a "Diva, female version of a Hustler, to the fullest". Every year she threw three parties in the summer time. [One at the beginning, another in the middle and one at the end. On the side, she would throw strip parties every other month at hotels for niggas.] Now is that a Hustler or what. Every Hustler's dream was to have a female like Meeka to build an empire with. I was just so lucky to have her as my sister.

Meeka and Monique came to see me faithfully, while I was in the State System, for that reason alone I owed them dearly. When I finally got on my feet the way that I wanted to, Meeka didn't have to want for nothing. Monique either, even though she was a successful Realtor and had her own money, I still bought and took her places whenever she could get away from her boyfriend.

I remember the week after I came home how I fucked the shit out of her. Let me rephrase that, she fucked the shit out of me.

Being that she took a two hour lunch break from her job that day, she called me and told me to meet her at the court yard hotel in Naptown.

When I got to room 112, Monique opened the door up with a long black silk robe that came down to her pretty little toes. Just looking at her beautiful smile, got me wondering what was underneath of that robe, and got my dick hard "immediately". After all them phone conversations and in the visiting room how she used to tease me, while I was up Jessup, I couldn't wait to fuck the shit out of her.

With a big cool aid smile on my face, I walked in and grabbed her from behind. The silk robe hugged her ass like it was painted on. My anaconda was very impatient, I unbuttoned my pants with one hand and quickly dropped them to my ankles. When I began to pull up her silk robe, Monique turned around then said,

"Wait!"

I said, "Wait for what?"

She saw the look on my face and started to laugh. I guess to her I looked some what like a sexual predator. I gave out a soft laugh then said,

"what's funny?"

Monique said, "take off all your clothes and walk in the bathroom".

I smiled then said, "alright".

While I stripped naked in front of the bathroom door, I thought about how she must want me to fuck her on the sink counter or in the shower. After I was ass naked, I turned around and looked at her and smiled.

While blushing she said,

"what you waiting for? . . . go in the bathroom".

Monique was shy, but she was a freak in the bed at the same time.

While I was walking into the bathroom, I cut my eyes at her and saw that she was blushing. I knew Monique long enough to know that was a sign to let me know that she had looked at my dick.

In the bathroom there were scented candles burning and a tub filled with water that had rose peddles floating around in it. To myself I said, "Damn, She went all out didn't she".

Monique walked in behind me, smacked me on the ass then said,

"get in the tub".

With a cool aid smile on my face, I looked at her then said,

"What you gonna do, wash me up?"

She said, "Hell yeah, you been home for a week, I don't know who you been with".

I said, "whatever . . . since you don't know where I been at, make sure you wash me up real good".

I got into the hot tub and relaxed myself so that I could begin to enjoy what she had in store for me. The scenery was like the movie "scarface", when Tony was sitting in the tub waiting to be catered to.

Monique grabbed the wash cloth and soap, got on her knees and began to wash my legs because she was to proud to wash my feet. After washing both of my legs separately, she observed my anaconda head peeking out of the water like a missle, Monique couldn't stop blushing. When she got to my upper thigh, she slowly rubbed up against my dick. I knew she was going to tease me before giving me the pussy just to make sure I was going to be pressed for more.

When she got to my waist, she rubbed up against my dick again then gave out a little laugh. After slowly washing my stomach, chest, arms, neck, and then my back she told me to stand up. When I stood up, the look on her face told me that her pussy was soak and wet. Monique got up off her knees with the soap and wash cloth in her hand and just smiled at me. She put her left hand on the bottom of my balls, then started stroking my dick with the soaky cloth. I tried to stand strong, but my dick had been hard for about 20 minutes now. I was unable to control myself any longer. When I came, the sperm shot up out of me like a python spitting venom at its predator. My legs began to buckle, I think I'm going into shock. When my legs gave out, I fell back to the wall to try to stop my fall.

Monique said, "Oh my god, are you ok?"

As I was sliding down the wall, I tried to talk, but nothing would come out. I believe I was slightly paralyzed. When my wet body made it all the way back into the tub, I came back to my senses. Monique rapped her arms around my neck then said,

"Booh, you alright?"

After I finally caught my breath I said,

"yeah . . . I'm good".

I smiled while looking at her. With her arms rapped around me she said,

"aww . . . the poor baby couldn't handle it?"

Then she started to laugh real loud.

With an embarrassed look on my face I said,

"whatever".

She said, "Damn, I'm almost scared to give you the pussy if you acted like that to a hand job".

I said, "you trying to show off huh?"

She blushed.

I said, "alright then . . . I'm ready to punish you".

She said, "oh, you must got your second wind now . . . action speaks louder than words".

When she walked out of the bathroom, she gave out another laugh.

As I was drying off, the only thing that was going through my mind was fucking the shit out of her ass. Fuck that, she wasn't going to leave from this hotel room thinking I couldn't even handle a hand job.

When I walked into the room, Monique had Beyonce's (Dangerously in Love) playing on the stereo and was standing by the bed. While smiling she said,

"I was beginning to think that you weren't coming?"

I smiled back then said,

"you really trying to show off ain't you?"

She said, "take that towel off and lay on the bed".

I cooperated. She got on the bed and stood over top of me while undoing her robe. I took both of my hands and put them behind my head while waiting for her to take me to ecstasy. My dick laid on my stomach like a full grown healthy banana. She took the robe off and threw it on the floor. Her C-cup size breast and that phat pussy made my dick go out of control. It repeatedly jumped and then smacked back at my stomach so hard that it looked as though it was choking on sperm. Monique stood there with her hands on her hips with the combination of a surprise and scared look on her face at the same time. Her pussy was so wet that it made her thighs shine from the reflection of the light.

I said, "don't get scared now?"

"Whatever". She replied.

Monique slowly squatted, grabbed my dick with her left hand then guided it through her pussy walls real slow. Once my dick head felt the hot wet juices, I was like a shark with the taste of blood in its mouth. While rolling her eyes into the back of her head, Monique slowly motioned up and down while putting me further and further inside her. I grabbed her hips and applied pressure downward so that she could speed the process up because I didn't know how long I was going to last until I exploded. I felt like a 40 year old virgin that was getting pussy for the first time, and all I wanted to do was relieve myself.

With a fragile voice she said,

"uh-oh, Hold up!"

With a smile on my face I said,

"what's wrong?"

All the shit she was talking in the bathroom, I was going to make her pay for sure.

Monique said, "let me do it, you just ain't going to jam all that in me like that".

I gave out a hyena laugh then said,

"yeah, you right".

She said, "smart ass".

With each motion of her hips, Monique got lower and lower. Her juices ran down my dick like an ice cream cone that had been sitting in front of a 100 degrees blistering hot sun.

While she tried to reach the goal of putting all of me up in her, she rolled her eyes while tilting her neck back with each downward motion. Once she was half way down, she must've realized that it was all she could take because she didn't allow me to go any deeper. While squatting and with both hands beside each side of my hips and her feet flat on the bed, she began to go full speed and get her "eagle on". The feeling was out of this world, I came instantly. She eagled my dick for about 20 minutes without stopping. In between Monique's screaming and moaning, she scratched my hips hard with her finger nails. Up and down, side to side. Her nice size breast flapped up against her upper stomach muscles as if they were making music together.

To me, Monique was a certified professional the way she moved her hips.

After I got that second climax I was paralyzed all over again. I couldn't move at all.

When she stopped, she looked at me and with her exhausting voice and said,

"you alright?"

"I'm good". I replied.

Still breathing hard she said,

"I'm not done yet".

I said, "finish what you started then".

Monique tried to give me one of her sexy blushes but couldn't because she was still out of breath.

After a couple of minutes of getting herself together, she spent around on my dick so that her ass was staring me in my face. With both of her hands on each side of my legs and with both of her feet flat on the bed, she started to get her eagle on again full speed. Up-down, up-down, side to side. From Monique's wet juices flowing out of her body, it made her ass clap together loud like it was applauding me for doing a good job. All that did was get me more motivated to tear her ass up. Every time she went down, I motioned her hips to go even deeper. She tried not to cooperate but she really didn't have a choice.

After we both went at it for about 15 minutes nonstop, I felt myself ready to climax. All the moaning and the scratching on my legs that she was doing, only motivated me more to try and put my full length inside her.

When that warm rush came over my body, I grabbed Monique's hips and used all my strength and forcefully push her all the way down on my dick.

"oh my god!", Monique screamed.

She looked back at me with her eyes wide open and said,

"Take it out, it's in my stomach!"

She tried to use her legs as springs so that she could bounce up off my dick, but it wasn't working. I had her body locked down on top of mine.

After I came, I got weaker and weaker. I couldn't pin her down no more. Monique jumped off and just stared at me while her fragile body rapidly shook. With a smile on my face I said,

"what's wrong?"

She said, "that shit ain't funny, you tried to hurt me!"

I said, "you should've thought about that before you started talking shit in the bathroom".

Monique laid on my body, we cuddled with each other while trying to catch our breath. We both held each other breathing heavy and sweaty, but satisfied. After about a half an hour Monique said,

"oh shit!"

I said, "what's wrong?"

She said, "I got to go back to work, I'm already late".

Monique jumped up and took a shower, I went out like a light. When I woke up there was a note beside me that read,

"call me later, and thank you".

That summer I took Monique to San Juan, Puerto Rico, she deserved it.

Being that it was my second time on an airplane, I wasn't as nervous as I was the first time.

[Puerto Rico was beautiful, but the people there weren't as nice to me as they were in Jamaica] We didn't pay them any mind because we went down there to enjoy ourselves and we weren't going to let anything stop us.

The scenery on the brand new sandals resort was lovely. All that hustling I was doing since I left the state system the past 10 months, it felt good to lay back and treat myself.

The sexy Porto Rican supervisor greeted us with a pretty Spanish smile and told us her name was "Maria".

Maria looked just like Jenifer Lopez, body and all. The only difference was that Maria had green eyes.

She gave us our credit cards and then checked us in. While taking us to our hotel room, Maria explained all the activities and events that were going to be happening on the resort.

When we got to our room, Maria informed us that our luggage would be coming shortly, and that if we needed anything to call up the front desk and ask for her. After giving me her sexy Puerto Rican smile, she walked off with her hair going one way and her ass going the other.

Our hotel room was nice, plus we had a beautiful view. When we walked out on the balcony we could see the whole ocean. Every night we spent in Puerto Rico, we sat on the balcony and watched the sun go down and the moon appear.

We've grown up with each other since we were in the sand box. When I looked into her eyes, I could tell that she loved me. I loved her too, but I wasn't ready to settle down yet. I was to deep into the game. I didn't want to feed her any broken promises. It was no telling when I was going to prison or somebody was going to put a bullet in my head. I was living day by day on the streets.

I guess that's one of the reasons why I respected why she was in a relationship with another person, because she deserves to be happy.

Monique had me thinking seriously about leaving the street life alone and settling down though.

I would sometimes think about having babies, so that I could see apart of me that wasn't always shady. But, if I had kids would I see them grow up. I didn't know because I lived a life of a hustler. I just spoiled all of the little project kids over Eastport like they were my own. When school time came around, I would buy shoes, school supplies for them, because I knew that their mothers were to busy on the streets getting high.

I knew if I would've told Monique that I was going to leave the street life alone and wanted us to start over again, she would have me. But, I wasn't ready yet, so I didn't want to put her through that.

Chapter 30

Business as Usual

When I got back to Maryland, I was pleased that Black had operated the family business successfully.

Black said, "while you were gone, Cheek-O, Fluid and some other people got locked up by the F.E.D.'s the other day".

I said, "Damn, shit was all good just a week ago".

Black said, "the F.E.D.'s confiscated the Cadillac truck and a lot of other shit from that nigga".

I said, "you win some, you lose some".

Black said, "I got word from some fiends that Bossman had been trying to get information about your where abouts".

I said, "fuck Bossman . . . that fat fuck can't stop me. I'm going to continue to rape Naptown, but this is just four play. I'm going to roll until the wheels fall off". My foot was sleeping on the gas pedal of a car with no brake pads, I was living life everyday like it was no tomorrow, then I'll do it all again like it was yesterday.

I had plans to take this drug game to a whole new level. I was going to make my mark in the Capital of Maryland that no other had made. The Annapoliteans were going to remember 'little Booh" one way or another.

Black said, "cousin -H wanted to get put on, and a nigga from Easton Shore name "Ron" came down and left a number for you to call him."

I said, "oh yeah, Eastern Shore Ron . . . that's the nigga I was locked up with when I was up Jessup. Call both of them niggas up and tell them to come holler at me."

I had about 15 different apartments over Eastport that I usually operated out of. The three fiends with the walkie talkies were posted up all day on each corner, so it was impossible for Dossman or anybody else to catch me or members of the family sleeping with our eyes closed.

[A couple of weeks later, I got my mother to co-sign for a townhouse for me. It was a nice three bedroom place in Arnold, right down the street from the community college]I got tired of spending nights with females at hotels, or staying at Sherica's house or Monique's down in the country.

I felt relieved to go to my house by myself and relax from a hard day at work.

Between the townhouse, car insurance, etc . . . I had crazy monthly bills that I was paying for, plus looking out for female family members that came around daily.

I decided to put my cousin H on, he was family, but wasn't selected as being in the family drug empire that I've hand picked.

-H was from up "Pioneer City". We used to beef with niggas from up there and "Mead Village" back when I was younger. Every time we would go and shoot-up Arwell court, I would call -H and make sure that he wasn't outside. Them niggas wasn't no worse though, they would come right back down Naptown just as strong.

[The nigga "Los" had that whole area on lockdown in the drug game for a while. He was a little hustler like me, who was also trying to live the American dream. Every time we saw each other at events, we always gave the other the proper respect. A couple of months ago he got "slumped" up in Glen Burnie.]

The problem that H had was that he loved to show off for the females. And that he always put his business second.

Skip taught me that, "you hustling backwards if your chasing a bitch . . . you stupid . . . chase the paper they come with it."

Two things that I've never seen, was a U.F.O. and a bitch I need. The only thing that I've ever chased was money, with the exception of Patron on a club night.

I convinced myself to give him a chance, but the first time he acted up, I was cutting him off. On the flip side, I wouldn't mind getting some of the niggas money up there.

When -H came to see me, he brought one of his flunkies with him. After we did business, I pulled him to the side and let him know that I didn't like extra company. After apologizing, he promised that it wasn't going to happen again.

When I walked outside to get some fresh air from cooking cocaine up half of the day I saw my man, "C-Doe".

C-Doe was from down the country, but he was adopted over Eastport and was buying weight from Black. He smoked so much weed that every time he talked it sounded like he was whispering.

C-Doe said, "Yo . . . that nigga with your peoples ain't right."

With a confused look on my face, I said,
"What you mean he ain't right?"

He said, "that niggas name is low, and he told on my peoples about a gun that had a body on it"

He said, "that nigga got my peoples life in prison . . . the only reason why I ain't slumped his ass was because he was with your peoples."

I gave C-Doe $500.00 for the information he just gave me. I called -H immediately and told him to come back and holler at me, "right now!"

When he came back, I informed him with the information I just got about the person he was with, He looked surprised and promised me that he was going to leave that nigga alone.

"Big-H" came home a couple of months later. I blessed him so that he could get on his feet because he was considered family and he was a soulja.

C h a p t e r   3 1

Present

L ittle-H hit the bunk then said,
"Stand up for count time yo"
I stood up then said,
"Damn, it's 3 o'clock already?"
"Yeah yo," he replied.

After the C.O's did their count, I got back on my bunk. Little-H said, "yo, I talked to my mother and she told me that my father be back at the Supermax in a couple of weeks." With a low voice I said, "yeah."

In my mind everybody was a suspect, especially Big-H because he got locked up a year before us by the F.E.D's. Little-H said, "niggas was down there earlier talking about why that nigga got killed this morning."

I said, "what they say?"

He said, "they say that the nigga had been a suspect for snitching . . . when niggas finally got proof that he helped the F.E.D.'s put together a 15 man indictment . . . that's why he got slumped."

"The 'Boca-Raton' was terrible," I replied.

Little-H said, "the nigga "Blew" from up 'Freetown' is over on F-4"
I said, "yeah!"

He said, "I was talking to him at the door."

I said, "I remember when I put out an expiration date on his head."

Little H said, "What ya'll was beefing on the streets?"

I said, "because $25,000 got stolen from one of my comrades stash house and that was the money that was owed to me. The little nigga told me that he got some legitimate information that a nigga name Blew from freetown took it."

Little H said, "I didn't know that."

I said, "I had a no tolerance rule when it came to the family and money."

He said, "what happened?"

I said, "I found out he didn't take the money . . . the little nigga cousin took it, so I called them hyenas off."

I sat there while Little H went on and on about how he should've figured out that the FED's was on him and the people he was around.

I wasn't really paying him any attention because the thought of him even talking about the situation got me mad.

After about and hour had passed, the C.O.'s saved me by popping the doors. I grabbed my chair and headed in the crowd of niggas so that I could get on the phone, soon I needed to call my grandparents house.

After about 10 minutes, I got on the phone and called and my mother answered the phone. With a fragile voice she said,

"how you doing Booh?"

I said, "I'm fine."

She said, "I talked to your lawyer and he said that he'll be over there to see you in a couple of weeks."

"Alright" I replied.

She said, "Hopefully your lawyer can get you another home monitor hearing."

I said, "don't get your hopes up high because the judge made it clear that I was a danger to the community."

She said, "how they going to give that other boy house arrest and he got caught in you alls indictment with 5 guns?"

I said, "because the boy low been working with the F.E.D's for a long time . . . the judge will consider me a danger to the community because the F.E.D.'s let the prosecutor know that I was a possible suspect in 3 murders over Eastport, so in the judges mind he's probably thinking that it won't take anything for me to get that nigga low and anybody else who I thought was telling 'slumped."

My mother sat quietly on the phone for a couple of seconds.

She said, "that's crazy how they could lock you up just because somebody said that you did something."

I said, "Conspiracy! That's just another way to let people know that the F.E.D.'s can do whatever and when ever they want to minorities."

She asked, "did you know the boy who got killed up there?"

I said, "I didn't know him, but it had something to do with snitching."

The 15 minutes seemed like it went so fast. I gave my mother some last minute instructions to give to Black and ensured her that I was ok.

Before hanging up the phone I said,

"I'll give you a call tomorrow."

She said, "I love you and that every body is praying for you."

I could hear the hurt in her voice, after I told her that I loved her too, the phone hung up. I took my chair and sat it next to Little-H, he said,

"how your mother taking it?"

"she holding up." I replied.

On the T.V. was the news, the spokes person talked about how the murder rate in Baltimore City had risen that year. Baltimore was the "murder capitol of the world, and you could tell from the news showing the daily slumping of niggas. Baltimore was also the "dope capital" of the world. The heroin brought a lot of jealousy and envy to "B-More Murdaland."

"Feed-Up! The ugly ass C.O. said. Her name was Ms. Ray, she looked like Whoopi Goldberg but was shorter, fatter and a head full of fake hair.

For dinner they gave us tasteless spaghetti with some watered down beans. I gave that shit to little-h and ate the cookies.

After the news went off, Ms. Ray yelled, "Doors Open!" I hurried up and ran to my cell and grabbed my shower stuff then headed to the shower, I waited in line for about a ½ hour until it was my turn.

The shower always smelled like piss, so before I would enter, I would run the water for a couple of minutes to try and get some of the smell out. I hurried and washed up because I knew Ms. Ray was on the way back to open the doors back up. Right after I dried off and stepped foot out of the shower, her ugly ass yelled, "doors open!"

It was going on 5 o'clock so I decided to stay in the cell for the rest of the day and go back into my thoughts.

Chapter 3 2

Living

At age 25, one would ask himself, "am I living or just existing?"
I was definitely living, and most of the credit went to the family,
because they played their positions and have proven to be loyal soulja's.
I had the whole family on Flip, like old box springs or pissy mattresses. I
made sure all of them were eating good, no cup of soups.

C was getting rid of two bricks a week down the country. C was
down the country running things.

Damien was getting rid of one brick a week up Baltimore off of
Monument street. Vedo was getting rid of a brick a week in P.G. County
off MLK.

Ron was over Eastern Shore getting rid of a brick a week, and little
H was up Pioneer city also selling a brick a week. They all were handling
their business like true hustlers.

As for the rest of the family, they had every project in Naptown in a
choke hold. Average, niggas was getting rid of 15-20 bricks a month for
me and was doing it with an "iron fist" Every brick they cooked-up they
would cut it so much that it would gain a half brick every time and the
product would still be fair. I had 75% of hustlers from Naptown buying
cocaine from me. Directly or indirectly, "supply and demand."

I knew this older black man that worked for this Fortune 500 company
for 25 years, a white man owned it, so the white man owned him. "Don't
nobody own me though," We all owe God a death, so in reality it's all
about how you going to alter your life before its time for you to pay up. I
got a lot of living to do before I die and I ain't have time to waste. Most

people fail in life not because they aim to high for a goal and miss, but they aim to low and hit."

My super optimism had kicked in and there was no turning back, I felt like I was untouchable, I was a local celebrity and was addicted to selling kilo's.

To treat myself I went to the dealership and bought a Range Rover, straight cash. When I took it off the lot, I drove straight up to Baltimore to "Wheel Deal" rim shop and bought some 20' Giovanni rims for it. When I drove around, it felt like I was driving on air. The hydraulics on the truck made it almost impossible for me to feel any bumps when I drove over top of them.

I felt like Harlem's own "rich porter" in my city. I would ride through the projects in Naptown, in one vehicle and then come right back through in something else. I had a vehicle for everyday of the week. You might say that I was being "cocky", but I would call it being "confident."

The late great Marcus Garvey once said, "if one doesn't have confidence in oneself, then he has already begun to have lost the fight, but if one has confidence in himself, then he has already begun to win the battle."

In my city, God only made a person like me every 10 years. That means that my competition is 10 years behind me. The only way that he'll ever catch up to me is if I slow down, and that was never going to happen, because I was on top of the hill. I guess this was how it felt to be rich. People say that Winning isn't everything, but it damn sure feels good.

I made the older hustlers wish for younger years, and the up and coming hustlers take notes so that they could start getting money like I was. Niggas in my city couldn't see me, but they could never over look me either.

I went up "ordinance road facility" to see my father, he was doing a year for another violation of probation.

When my father walked out to the visitor's booth, he smiled from cheek to cheek.

He said, "What's up son?"

I said, "ain't nothing, chilling."

My father looked at me with proudness on his face, he was happy to see his son living successfully in the cold world. He said, "son, your name been ringing all through the jail, and everybody act like they know you." I said, "yeah I'm doing ok for myself."

He said, "all I hear is good things about you . . . everybody speaks so highly about you in here."

I said, "I learned from you when I was growing up . . . you told me if I wanted respect that I had to earn it."

My father just looked at me and smiled. We reminisced about the past for about an hour. When the visit time was over with, my father told me that he loved me and to be careful out there on the streets. I sent him my love also and told him to keep his head up.

Big-H paged me and left a message saying that he needed to talk to me. It sounded important so I called and told him to meet me up Glen Burnie in the Taco Bell parking lot. When I pulled up at the restaurant, Big-H walked out with a bag full of food. I pulled up beside him and he jumped in my truck.

He said, "Damn, this motha fucka's nice yo!"

I said, "Thanks"

He said, "yo did you send that nigga 'Maudy' to my job to holler at me about buying some coke?"

I said, "hell nawh! That nigga told you that?"

"Yeah" he replied.

I said, "my brother told me not too long ago that Maudy was snitching."

Big H said, "I'm going to call him up later on today and tell him to come holler at me . . . when he come I'm a write everything down on paper just in case he is working with them "peoples" (F.E.D.'s).

I said, "that's up to you, but I think that you should leave that nigga alone?"

Big-H said, "on other things . . . I got a connect up New York, so if you ever need some good coke let me know."

I smiled then said, "I'm good, I got my glasses on waiting for the sun to shine."

That was another thing that I've learned in the drug game, "if it ain't broke then don't fix it." What I look like cutting my connect off and start buying from him, I mess around and get caught up in some dumb shit. Regardless of what the price of the Kilo's are, "all money ain't good money."

The next day I got a call from Pack-O telling me that I had a violation of Probation Warrant on me. I thought to myself, "damn, I haven't got locked up for anything so why the fuck I got a warrant on me." Since I came home from up Jessup, I been reporting to my P.O. every month, and all my drug tests been clean.

I called Peter O'Neel and he informed me that the violation had a set "no bail" on it, and I'm more than likely going to have to go to D.O.C for a hearing. I told O'Neel, once he get information on what the violation was for let me know.

I went to my townhouse and relaxed for the rest of the day, just the thought of how much money I'll miss for being locked up made me upset.

Later that day O'Neel called my cell phone.

He said, "your parole officer said that an anonymous person called him and told him that you went out of state not to long ago."

I said, "what!"

He said, "Mr. Zelco says he did some investigation and it all checked out that your I.D. was used to go to Puerto Rico a little while back . . . he also stated that rule #3 states that you are not to leave the state without notifying your probation officer."

I said, "what can you do to make this disappear?"

He said, "I can't do anything about this situation because it's a parole violation . . . . the best thing you should do is turn yourself in so that you can get this past you."

I said, "how long am I going to be gone for?"

He said, "the process might only take no more than a month"

I said, "Damn, that's a lot of money I'm going to miss."

O'Neel said, "its not a serious violation . . . so plead guilty . . . the state system is so over crowded that they'll more then likely release you back into society."

The next week, I went down to the Harbor to meet Diablo as usual. Earlier that week I called Blonco and told him the situation about me having to leave for a month or two. I told him to double the package of Kilo's and I assured him that his money was in good hands, he agreed.

C h a p t e r 3 3

M.C.I.J.

I turned myself in at the police station a couple of days later. I made sure that Black had all the instructions and directions to run my operation while I was gone. The ride to D.O.C. was short. After going through the procedure, I got sent to my tier.

My cell buddy was a little nigga named "Steve". He was from over Greenmount, off of 20th and Kennedy. He also was at the D.O.C. for a violation.

[Steve broke the law down to me about the whole parole violation process. He told me that in a couple of weeks that the committee would decide whether to send my case to "M.C.I.J." (Maryland Correction Institution Jessup) or send me back into society. Steve said that they were going to send me home simply because I didn't break any laws while I was out of town. After hearing that I felt good because that meant I could be back on the streets in no time.]

*[He was wrong though, D.O.C. had me on the first thing smoking up Jessup.

M.C.I.J. was a medium security prison that was slowly transforming into a parole retake facility. I stayed in "J Dorm." The tier was medium size. It had two TV's and a laundry room down stairs which was really used as a "war zone" for the inmates.

*[It seemed like everybody was beefing with each other. Bloodz was beefing with the Muslims, and the B.G.F. was beefing with any and everybody who ever tried to disrespect their cash flow that was coming inside of the prison.

This was another killing field that I got sent too. I was beginning to believe that it probably was meant for me to be killed in the penal system.

While I was walking to my dorm, a nigga grabbed my shoulder then said, "what's up shorty?"

The first thing that went through my mind was that I haven't been on the compound for an hour yet and I already got to chop a nigga up. I turned around and "Neak" said, "hold up shorty, it's me."

I said, "yo, I didn't know who you were."

[Neak was a Yankee (N.Y.) nigga who was buying weight from my brother, plus he was a C.O. at M.C.I.J.]

Neak said, "yo, your brother told me you was on the way up here . . . let me know what you need."

I said, "I need some tobacco to sell so that I could buy some commissary to hold me over after dry week (inventory)"

Neak said, "I bring it when I come back to work tomorrow . . . watch these niggas up here because it's a lot of telling going on."

I said, "yo you don't have to worry about me talking about what business we do . . . ain't nothing changed, I'm the same nigga on the streets."

My bunk buddy was a big country dirty ass white boy with stringy hair named, "Jumb." He was from out Harford county and was at M.C.I.J. for a violation also. He informed me that it'll take between 2-4 weeks to go up for a violation hearing, and that it was a good chance that they'll send me back into society because of the over crowded prison.

Besides the snoring and talking about how high he used to get, he was ok.

The next day when Neak brought me the tobacco, I hit Jumbo off but told him don't smoke while I was in the cell.

I called Black that next week to make sure everything was going as planned with my business. When he answered the phone I could hear it in his voice that something was wrong. He informed me that somebody had taken two kilo's out of the trunk of his old car that was parked outside of his apartment. He also informed me that the two suspects who he had in mind were "Zeeto and Grick." They both were some grimy ass niggas that couldn't be trusted. They must have gone crazy to ever steal from me.

The family members and me never really had beef with niggas, because the ones who knew us knew the reputation that had spoke for itself.

The family was behind me 100% when beefing, we weren't satisfied until your mother got that phone call from the doctor. Then it was even.

I told Black to chill, don't worry about it, I'll handle it when I get back home. This kind of disrespect had to be handled like chess and not checkers.

This situation was one of the reasons why the world was filled with shadows now, because it's always somebody trying to stand in the way of a nigga's shine.

The next 3 weeks had dragged along for me because just the thought of somebody disrespecting the family kept my blood pressure at a high level.

The C.O. popped my cell door at 7am that morning of my violation hearing. When I got into the room, I saw my P.O. and a woman who looked like Angela Basset with short hair. Her name was Ms. Nancy and she was the one who was going to make the decision on my hearing.

Ms. Nancy introduced herself then said,

"you should already know your P.O. Mr. Zelco"

I said, "yeah I know him," with the look of disgust on my face. Mr Zelco just sat there and smiled.

Ms. Nancy said, "Mr Walders, you are in violation of parole for leaving the state . . . how do you plea?"

I said, "guilty."

Ms. Nancy looked at Mr. Zelco then asked,

"Is there anything that you would like to add before I make my decision?"

He said, "Mr. Walders has been seeing me on a regular basis and he's been given clean urine every time."

I thought to myself, damn this fat pig act like he want me to go home.

Ms Nancy said, "Mr. Walders . . . I'm going to release you back to society, but if you come back in front of me for any reason, you'll be staying in prison for the remainder of your sentence."

I said, "yes mam, thank you!"

I had to thank her, because she just made the decision to send me back to society so that I could continue to run my business.

Once I got back to the block and called Black to come pick me up, my whole mood had changed because the thought of someone taking something from me was fucking with me "mentally." Zeeto and Grick were into everything except a casket, but I was going to see if I could make that happen for them.

I walked out of M.C.I.J at about 2 pm that same day with pants on that had the D.O.C. stamp on the pant leg, white t-shirt and some fake ass state shoes. While riding down highway 97, Black said,

"niggas must have plotted and saw me put the kilos in the stash car."

I said, "you sure it was them niggas who did it?"

He said, "two different people separately saw both of them niggas around the car late that night . . . you want me to call Muse to tell him to get them hyenas ready?"

I said, "Nawh, I'm going to handle this myself."

He said, "besides that situation everything else was going as planned."

I said, "as it should, it wasn't a doubt in my mind that you couldn't run the business while I was away."

I called Blonco and got back on track with him like a pair of Pumas. It was like I hadn't missed a beat.

Chapter 34

"Get It How You Live"

Skip came home from the "cut" after doing 3 ½ years. I showed him the proper love and respect that a father figure deserved.

Skip said, "Shorty, I been hearing your name ringing real loud while I was away."

I smiled because the feeling that I felt was when a father tells his son how proud he was of him. The expression on his face let me know that he felt as though he saw his son succeed in life.

Skip said, "you remember your promise to me, right?"

I smiled because I knew what he was getting at.

I said, "yeah . . . . I promised you that after I've reached $100,000.00 that I was going to call it quits."

Skip said, "I know that you been over that six figure line . . . so why you still hustling?"

I said, "I'm seeing to much money now . . . plus I got too many responsibilities to ever try and leave the game."

With a serious look on his face he said,

"what responsibilities do you have?"

I said, "I'm responsible for my brother and my cousins . . . if I just jump-up and quit, it's like leaving them stranded . . . you always taught me that with power comes responsibility."

I could literally see the anger in his face. It was the same look when a parent tells their child not to touch the hot iron because by knowledge they don't want to see their child get burned.

Skip said, "You ain't responsible for those niggas. They grown men and as for the money, I told you when you first started playing, that people get so focused on growing in the game they forget why their in it. Effort and courage isn't enough to be successful, in the game you need purpose and direction. It makes no difference how much money your making, if you don't have a vision or a goal, it's only going to be a matter of time before the streets swallow you up."

I was ashamed, I knew he was telling the truth. I've been raped by the drug game in Naptown ever since I was about 12 years old, you could have called it statutory rape.

I said, "I'm going to ride it out until next summer, then I'll call it quits." Knowing in my heart I wasn't going to divorce the game, I was in her too deep. Me leaving the drug game alone at that point in my life was almost like disowning my last name. I had to keep feeding the streets in my city, because it had a starving appetite. It wasn't going to happen. Skip gave me a fatherly hug, then said, "don't get it twisted because the game ain't sweet. Life's a bitch and then you die, but the money will make you forgive it. Remember this Shorty, in the heat of victory, arrogance and over confidence can push you pass the goal or vision that you had aimed for, and by going pass your goal or vision you start making more enemies then you defeat. You got to be true to yourself and never forget where you came from, because at the top, the air is real thin, it'll be hard for your ass to breath sooner or later you'll be just another statistic."

Skip gave me the drug game when I was coming up, but now he was telling me to get out because the only thing that's worse then getting old is not getting old.

[The family members and I decided to go up "Bill Dotson" for my birthday to have a couple of drinks and unwind.]

Bill Dotson was a hole in the wall that was in the Glen Burnie area, we didn't care though because there was always females up there. The club was so small that you had to bump and rub shoulders everywhere inside.

[I got a call from over Eastport informing me that Zeeto just got slumpted and Grick got shot up real bad about an hour ago. The caller told me that if that nigga Grick didn't die by the end of the night, then he's going to wish that he was dead. I hung up the phone then to myself I said, "Checkmate . . . . get it how you live."]

The next day I went over Eastport to do my regular rounds. Just my luck, I happened to run into Bossman and his flunky on Sanky street. When I walked out of the store, they were waiting for me.

I said, "Fuck ya'll want now?"

Bossman said, "put your hands behind your back."

"For what," I replied

While the flunky patted me down he said,

"For murder and attempted murder"

While the handcuffs were being put on me I said,

C'mon Bossman, when ya'll gonna stop trying to charge me with bullshit that ya'll know I ain't do?"

While I was being put in the back seat of the police car Bossman said,

"Oh we know that you probably didn't do it, but you got somebody to do it for you."

I let out a fake hyena laugh.

While riding down BayRidge to homicide, Bossman said, "I know you got Zeeto killed and Grick shot the fuck up for taking those two kilos of cocaine from your brother."

I sat in the backseat and said nothing, they already knew that I was going to give them the silent treatment. Down at homicide, I was being interrogated for what seemed like 4 hours. After I repeatedly asked to call my lawyer and them calling me every racial name in the book, they finally called it quits.

Bossman literally pushed me out of the door then said,

"Find your own way back to the jungle, monkey!"

Bossman sat behind his desk and let out a deep exhale. He said, "out of all the years I been working on these streets, I believe that little Booh is the only nigger that gets underneath my skin."

The flunky said, "don't worry about it Boss . . . that nigger's going to get what's coming to him . . . sooner or later."

The phone started to ring, the flunky picked it up.

"Hello!"

"Yes I'm agent Thomas with the DEA and I'm looking to speak to an officer Bossman."

The flunky said,

"Boss there's a federal agent Thomas on the phone that wants to speak with you."

Bossman lifted up from the chair and grabbed the phone.

"Yeah, this is Bossman."

Thomas said, "Officer Bossman, I was told by your supervisor that you're the person to talk to about a drug dealer in your city name 'little booh'"

"What do you want to know about him?"

Thomas said, "I have a C.I. (confidential informant) that's telling me that [Mr. Walders is supplying drugs to a gang that I'm investigating known as the "Pioneer City Boys"]

Bossman smiled, then let out a loud laugh. This was the break that he had been waiting for. To him it was almost the same as someone calling and telling him that they've finally found the person who sold his daughter the crack that killed her.

Thomas said, "what's funny?"

Bossman leaned back in the chair, kicked his feet up on the desk then said, "You just made my day. I hope you got a pen and notebook because I'm going to tell you any and everything I know about his little ass."

Chapter 35

Million Dollar Dreams and Federal Nightmares

2004 had come and gone, and 2005 was finally here. The family was still standing strong and Blonco always got his money on time.

I picked my father up at the Ordinance Road Facility at 10 o'clock that morning. When he saw the Range Rover, his eyes looked like they were about to pop out of his head. With a smile on both of our faces, we both greeted each other with happiness. My father was happy to see the truck because that was proof that things he had heard about his son were true. I was happy to see my father come home, especially while I was at the top of my game. I would be able to take care of him the way I wanted too.

We spent the whole day together. After taking him shopping, I gave him $1,000 later that day then dropped him off down in the country.

Being successful in the drug game was nothing without enjoying yourself. I took Monique with me to the M.C.I. Center in D.C. to the Mike Tyson fight.

I was never one of those type of people to sit in the house and watch sports or study another person's career. I used my spare time trying to brain storm on how I can make millions like them. Since the fight was so close to home, I made an exception.

I was dressed in a linen off white outfit, bubble gum gator shoes, with the bubble gum gator belt. Monique had on a Gucci dress with some Gucci shoes. To top it all off I rented a Lexus limousine for the night, couldn't nobody tell us anything.

At the M.C.I. Center, we were escorted to our $1,500 seats in the celebrity section. "Bishop Don Juan" was seated in front of us, he agreed and let Monique take a picture of me and him together. Every time Monique and I got a chance, we had anybody that we could get to take pictures of us, because this was a night to remember.

The center was packed with celebrities. The only famous person that I got star struck over was the great "Muhammad Ali." When he walked into the center, everybody clapped, got to their feet and showed the proper respect that the GREATEST deserved. Ali came to the show with his daughter "Leila Ali" for support, she was also on the fight card.

After Leila punished her opponent and the Irish boxer made Mike Tyson quit, we called it a night and got the limousine to drop us off at our hotel room in Naptown.

Life was going good for me, but I kept having this feeling in my gut that something wasn't right, and I just couldn't put my finger on it. It felt like I was still being cheated, for the first time in my life I was getting money, but it was like my conscience was eating me up.

I gave O'Neel a call the next day to ask for his opinion on a Federal lawyer.

O'Neel said, "What do you need a federal lawyer for?"

I said, "I need a professional opinion on a matter . . ."

O'Neel said, "If someone in my family needed a federal lawyer, I would send them to "Larry Natans" . . . we've been friends for so long and more importantly I trust him . . . my opinion, he's the best federal lawyer in Baltimore City."

O'Neel gave me the number and told me he'll call Larry to confirm that I'm a client of his.

I needed a federal lawyer because I knew that I was bigger than the state system. I'm not a child, I needed nothing for security, but I needed a federal lawyer in case the "big boys" start getting nosey.

People have been getting locked up with the FEDS left and right over Eastport, and I know my name had been brought up in at least one of those situations.

I knew that any criminal charges that Annapolis City gave to me I could hire O'Neel to beat it, but fucking with the FEDS was a dangerous game to be played. I knew people that got sent to the FEDS and were never to be seen again.

I called Larry and set an appointment with him for a couple of days later. When I got to the building in East Baltimore, I took the elevator to the 3rd floor to Larry's office. His secretary told me that he'd be with me in a minute.

Her name was "Lisa" and she looked like Jessica Simpson with some sexy glasses on. She never did stand up, she was always behind the desk so I never did get a good look at the body.

After waiting for a short while, Larry came out and greeted me with a hand shake after introducing himself.

He said, "Mr. Walders I've talked to Peter O'Neel a couple of days ago . . . I've been expecting you.

I followed Larry into his office, where he signaled me to have a seat.

Larry asked, "What can I do for you?"

I said, "is there anyway that you can find out if I'm being investigated by the FEDS?"

Larry said, "The only way that I can find out is if you hire me as your lawyer and I'll start filing some motions. Is there any reason why you think that federal agents are investigating you?"

I said, "some situations have been going on in my city for some time now and I just want to be two steps ahead of anything that's coming my way."

Larry said, "first, before I become your lawyer, you've got to trust me."

I said, "ok"

Knowing in the back of my head, there ain't no way I was going to trust this white man. I was going to trust him to do what I wanted him to do.

✶ [Larry said, "my fee starts off at $75,000 and if you do receive a federal charge, the money would be a start up fee for your case . . . and if you decide to go to trial, its going to be extra."

I said, "ok"

He said, "If you don't get a federal case within 10 years, your fee is gone and I'm no longer your lawyer.]

I said, I could deal with that, and I'll drop the money off tomorrow."

Larry said, "give me a second while I get my secretary to type up a contract."

I said "alright."

When Larry left the room I observed the medals of success, college degrees, and newspaper articles that he had in his office. He was the chairman of his law firm and was known nationwide.

When Larry walked back into the room he said,

"Mr. Walders I'll see you tomorrow, on your way out of my office my secretary has some papers for you to sign."

"thank you," I replied

I walked to Lisa's desk and she had the contract waiting for me to sign. She gave me her sexy Jessica Simpson smile, then said,

"Here's your papers and if you have any questions call the office and ask for me."

The next day I took the money and the contract to Larry. He assured me that he'd stay in touch.

C h a p t e r   3 6

It Comes With The Game

It was the beginning of the summer and everything was going as planned. The family and I continued to run the city with an "iron fist."

My clientele had blown up so much that I had to call Blonco and tell him to add an extra 10 Kilo's to my package. He was so happy to hear that he lowered the price on them. The 50 kilo's of Cocaine I was getting, was going for $22,000 a piece. I lowered the price to the family, but everybody else got it for the same price as before. I was a "Bonefied Hustler", I was planning on riding until the wheels fell off.

I was so far ahead of my time, I was about to start another life, I told niggas to look behind them because I was about to pass them twice.

To treat myself, I bought another old school antique car. After getting it painted I rimed it, and I took it up to Baltimore to a white boy shop on "O'Donnell street" and paid them $7,500 to put some Lamborghini doors on it. Being the first person in Maryland with an antique car with lambo doors, you know that I had to show it off. That same night I picked my car up, I road through every projects in Naptown with the doors up. Whatever people were doing when I drove through, the stereo system got their attention and when they saw how the car looked, there mouths were wide open, like on that Fabulous video "Breath".

Instead of getting high off of drugs, I got high off of life. I loved the attention, there was no better feeling.

My pager started vibrating about 1 o'clock that morning. Sherica pushed my shoulder then said,

"one of your bitches calling you".

I said, "Whatever".

Lately she'd been complaining about me going out of town and staying out late. I was treating my last like my first, and my first like my last, and the last the same way when I first started to play in the Drug Game.

That's what's wrong with a lot of females who are in relationships with so called "stars" who were playing in the Game. They enjoyed living the fabulous life style, but didn't want to take everything else that came with it. There's no such thing as being halfway in the Game, either you in it or you're in the way. If you spending any of that drug money, driving or got any of them vehicles in your name you best believe, if the FED's snatch your man up, you more than likely going to take that ride with him.

When I picked my pager up, I saw little-One's called 911 behind it. I immediately called him, when he answered the phone I could tell that something was wrong.

I said, "what's wrong yo!"

He said, "niggas just robbed me".

I said, "Who!"

He said, "some lame niggas?"

I said, "you know who they were?"

He said, "Yeah. Crack head "Stewy" set me up".

I said, "you sure?"

He said, "positive".

I said, "don't do anything. Go in the house for the night and I'll see you tomorrow".

He said, "alright".

After hanging up the phone, I sat there and thought to myself, "I know that nigga Stewy ain't bumped his head. It had to be more to it because I know he wouldn't disrespect the family like that ". Stewy use to wash my cars and go anywhere in Naptown for me, if I needed him to. More importantly, he and everybody who knew me knew that I had a no-tolerance rule when it came to disrespecting the family.

After dropping Sherica off at work the next morning, I went over EastPort to holler at Stewy to see what was going on. When I got over there I saw the police yellow tape in front of the building 1175.

Annie-May was the only person outside at the time in the project.

I said, "Annie-May, what happened over here?"

With her stale crackly voice she said,

"you ain't heard?"

In a smart voice I said,

"If I heard what happened I wouldn't have asked your ugly ass".

She said, "Stewy got killed."

With a surprise look on my face I said,

"for real!"

Annie-May said, "people saying that you had something to do with it because your peoples got robbed".

With anger in my voice I said, How the fuck I have something to do with it, when I just asked you what happened?"

She said, "don't kill the messenger, that's just what people saying".

I knew once Bossman heard about this, he was going to come looking for me.

I called Little-one and the rest of the members of the family to see if they had something to do with Stewy getting slumped, all of them swore that they had nothing to do with the situation.

I walked down Sanky's store to get my usual, as soon as I walked out of the store guess who was waiting for me? Bossman and the Flunky.

I hurried up and drunk the orange juice because I knew I was about to go down homicide

Bossman gave me his famous joker smile while swinging the hand cuffs in his hand. After I threw the juice bottle in the trash, I smiled, then put my hands behind my back.

Down Homicide, after going through the usual procedure for about an hour, they decided to call it quits. This time was different though, for some strange reason they weren't mad at me or abusive like they used to be.

Bossman pushed me out of the Homicide building then said, "have a nice day", while giving me the smile of death. Right then I knew that poor white trash and his flunky was up to something.

The next week little-H came to see me to inform me that his father got locked up by the FED's the other night.

I said, "what happened!

He said, "that nigga "Maudy" set him up and got his house knocked"

I said, "I told your father, leave that nigga alone".

He said, "I know yo".

I said, "what the FED's get out the house?"

He said, "they got $31.000, a brick of crack and an ounce of powder".

I said, "Damn!"

With a sad look on his face he said, "I know yo".

I said, "let your mother know I'm going to drop some money off to go towards his lawyer".

He said, "ok".

Big-H was doing his own thing, if he was on my team 100%, I wouldn't have any problem paying a lawyer in full for him, but he wasn't. See, if I was blind to the Game and decided to cut my connect off and start buying from him, I would've been in the same situation he was in right now. Like I said, "all money ain't good money".

After little-H re-uped, I asked him,

"you leaving that nigga "low" alone?"

He said, "yeah, I don't fuck with that nigga no more".

I said, "good".

Later that day I got a call from Federal lawyer Larry, as soon as I heard his voice on the other end of the phone I knew that it was bad news. Larry told me that he needed me to come to his office as soon as possible.

The ride to Baltimore was so nerve racking because I was so worried about what kind of bad news Larry had for me.

When I got to the office, Lisa greeted me with that same Jessica Simpson smile, she didn't get the usual attention from me because I had other important things on my mind.

Larry came out and greeted me, then escorted me to his office. When I took a seat, he put some papers on his desk, looked at me then took a deep breath.

He said, "Mr. Walders, federal agents have teamed up with Annapolis city police officers and started an investigation on you".

With a dumb look on my face I said, "oh yeah?"

Larry handed me some papers then said, "when you read these papers your going to see that the FED's called Annapolis police and got a lot of information on you. Annapolis officers informed the FED's that you are a "Major Drug Dealer" and that you are considered "Mr. Untouchable", because they never could catch you doing anything illegal".

As I read the papers, I saw that Bossman and his flunky were the top two officers working with the FED's. I knew that they were up to something after that last run in I had with them. While I continued to read the rest of the papers, the only thing that got my attention was that I was named a suspect in three homicides in the city of Annapolis.

I asked Larry, "what was the reason why the FED's started their investigation?"

He said, "I'm not going to be able to get that kind of information because it could damage their case".

The rest of the day I sat in my town house and thought long and hard about what could've started my investigation. I know that it was a good possibility that niggas were singing like birds, but I knew that it had to be more to it. All this was telling me was to keep my circle tight and watch what I say on the phone. A.P.D never caught me with anything, and I was for damn sure not going to let the FED's catch me with anything either.

The next week I got a call from little-H telling me that he had to see me, I told him to come holler at me down Naptown-20. He just re-uped with me the other day, so either his father needed more money for his lawyer or something was wrong. Half an hour later, I met little-H in the parking lot. When I got to the passenger side of what looked like a fiend's car, we greeted each other.

He said, "I talked to my father and he said the night that he got locked-up, the FED's was trying to ask him questions about you and that they wanted you real bad".

I said, "don't even worry about that, niggas been telling on me for years now and ain't nothing happened yet. I'm to smart for them, they will never catch me with any drugs on me".

Little-H said, "my father appreciated the money for the lawyer and he told me to tell you to be careful".

I said, "on other things, when the last time you saw that nigga "low?"

He said, "we just went out to Bill Dotson last week".

With anger in my voice I said,

Yo, I thought I told you to leave that nigga alone?"

He said, "nawh-yo, I don't do no business around him, we just go out to clubs every now and then".

I said, "Stop being so fucking stupid. Leave that nigga alone all the way! If he was working with the FED's, he's going to keep feeding them information and the investigation is going to continue. That's food for thought, now you do the dishes".

That nigga had me so mad that I left up out his face without showing no love.

CHAPTER 37

The Close's Distance Between Two People Is Communication

That Saturday morning I went to "Divas Hair Salon" to get my dreads twisted. Just like another salon, it was a gossip spot. I didn't care though because I enjoyed the way the females would switch their asses a little harder when they saw me watching them. Ever since I came home, I would get my hair done twice a month by "Teisha".

Teisha was around my age and was from down "Bywaters". She looked and was built like Keisha Cole without the gap in her mouth.

The one thing that niggas in Naptown would agree on is that females from down Bywaters were from a different bread then your average project chick.

In every project in Naptown you got a couple of dimes walking around looking sexy, them bitches be broke though. Most of them ain't got 10 pennies to their name. They looking for a come up. Anybody that's getting money in the Drug Game, these females preyed on them. If that Hustler go to jail or go broke, them bitches be after the next person in line that was playing the game.

The Bywaters females dressed and carried themselves in a different way. A lot of them had their own houses, a good job and weren't out on the streets in everybody's business.

While doing my hair Teisha said, "Booh, you heard what happened last night at the club in Odenten?"

I said, "nawh what happened?"

She said, "them dumb ass Pioneer City niggas shot a police up there last night".

I said, "What!"

She said, "Yeah"

Teisha filled me in on how little-H and his crew were taking pictures at the club with real guns out like they was "Alpo" on the movie "Paid in Full".

I couldn't believe what the fuck I was hearing. I called little-H up on the phone and told him to come and see me immediately and bring that couple of dollars with him.

Little-H met me over Harbor House a couple of hours later in front of the 1165 building. When I sat down on the passenger seat, I looked at him and said,

"Yo, what the fuck is wrong wit you?"

He looked at me with a sad look on his face and said,

"Yo, them niggas crazy".

I said, "you right with them. Where that money at?"

Little-H reached in the back seat and grabbed a small plastic trash bag.

He said, "I'm a have to owe you $3,500".

I said, "this $27,500?"

He said, "yeah"

I told him to call me as soon as he get the rest of the money. I got up out of the car without even showing him any love. I didn't even have to tell him because he knew that he was "cut off" for being so dumb and stupid. I couldn't let that nigga and his crew put my family in jeopardy.

The following week, Black, C-doe, and about ten Hyenas and me, went up to Owings Mills to "Gellians".

*[Gellians was the spot on Saturday nights. Females from all over used the club as a fashion show and to see what niggas they could catch. Where there were females, there were niggas. Every time we went up there, we took the "Alphabets and numbers" with us just incase anybody decided to act-up.

That particular night was fight night, Bernard Hopkins vs Trinadad. Gellians was jammed packed, the line seemed like a mile long. We weren't trying to wait in line though. We walked to some females that were close to the entrance and told them that we'd pay their way in and buy them drinks all night long if they let us cut in front of them. After flirting with them for a couple minutes, they agreed. We observed niggas twisting their faces up because we cut in front the line, but they didn't say anything though. They didn't want to feel the vibe of our mothers corrupted seed. Fuck around and have their homies burning a "rest in piece" candle.

When we got into the club area, we went straight to the bar, got something to drink and then went and posted-up in the back. C-doe leaned towards me, pointed then said,

"Yo, ain't that nigga "low" right there?"

I looked towards the direction he was pointing and said, "that is that snitch ass nigga".

C-doe said, "I'm a go over there and smack the shit out of him like the bitch nigga he is".

I said, "chill yo. We gonna wait until towards the end before punishing him".

For all I knew, he was the main reason why the FED's were investigating me.

After the club area closed down for the night, we posted up by the pool table and waited on that nigga. Low had to walk past us because that was the only way out of the club.

C-doe tapped my shoulder and said, "there that nigga go right there".

I said, "I'm a pop the shit out of him first, then y'all can go on and do what y'all do best".

Low walked out like he had no worries in the world, when he looked up and locked eyes with me, it was too late. I popped the shit out of him and before he hit the ground Black, C-doe and the rest of the niggas with us were on him like a bunch of wild Hyenas. By the time the security guards got there, that nigga looked like a piece of beaten meat.

I knew the FED's weren't going to take to kindly that one of their informants got fucked up by some niggas that they are investigating.

C H A P T E R   3 8

Victory Lap

All that night while lying in my bed, I thought about all the things that I've done, and all of the things that I'll probably do, if I continued to hustle. The streets were killing me, but at the same time keeping me alive. One would've never known because I always stayed nonchalant.

The next day when I woke-up, the first thing I did was call Blonco to let him know what was going on. He agreed that it was best to chill for about six months until things died down. I met Diablo the following week to give the money from the last package.

I called Meeka so that she could find me somewhere out of state to stay for a little while. After I explained the situation to her, she immediately went on the computer and found me a spot down North Carolina. I figured that I could come back to Maryland every month to see my P.O., so it shouldn't be any problem. Meeka and my mother were the only people at the time that knew that I was leaving, both were sad but they knew it was the best thing for me to do.

I called everybody in the family and told them to meet me over Eastport at the spot at 5pm.

When I walked in Annie-May's house, everybody who was supposed to be there was there. I gave Annie-May a gram of crack and told her, take a walk.

I looked at my family and then took a deep breath

I said, "I called this meeting to let y'all know I'm out of the game".

Black said, "what you mean you out?"

I said, "I'm done. Game Over".

Damon said, "why, from that shit that happened up at the club?"

T-Bone said, "give me the word yo, I'll make sure that nigga don't see the end of the summer".

I said, "it ain't that easy, That nigga working with the "Big Boys" so you know they watching him".

Little-One looked at me and said,

"you serious yo?"

I looked at my protégé and said,

"Shorty, when you in a position like I'm in, you know when it's time to call it quits".

Black said, "who we suppose to buy weight from now?"

I said, "after things die down in about six months, I'll jump back into the game, but until then I'm done".

C said, "Booh, I'm a just buy weight from other niggas just to stay a float down the country".

I said, "that's what I want y'all to do, go try and find other connects so that y'all don't go broke. I know the quality and the prices ain't going to be the same, but y'all still need to survive".

After spending about an hour explaining to the family why I was calling it quits, I finally got their approval.

Without hustling, my days dragged on and on. Financially, I was well off because the money that I've made from the Drug Game could've lasted me for two lifetimes if I spent it right. I swore to myself that when I left this earth it was going to be on both feet and never knees in the dirt. Mentally, I was fucked-up. I wasn't use to sitting around doing nothing. Many of the times I thought about all the obstacles and marathons in the game that I've completed, I guess this was the "Victory Lap". I was emotional because I loved the block. I missed the Drug Game, but in my heart I knew this was the right thing to do.

August came and I was about a month clean of not fucking with the game. Black was maintaining, he was supplying the family by buying some garbage Cocaine from Baltimore stars.

It seemed like the whole Naptown was in Chaos, everybody and their mother was looking for Drugs. I realized right then and there, I've made a major mark on the Capital of Maryland. I left niggas on injured reserve in my city, that's how much hurting I had put on the game. I set my city on fire and I didn't even try. I had plans to keep running the streets all day and sleep when I die. I fucked the drug game in Naptown until it constantly gave me money. The feeling had me in ecstasy.

I was the "One on One", that means none before it, and none to come Drug dealer that the Capital of Maryland had ever seen thus far. If the drug game in my city was a painting, I would be Mozart because them other hustlers was just tracing over what I had already done. Often imitated, but never duplicated.

While the Drug Dealers in Naptown felt like it was the end of the world, the people in New Orleans were going through the real disaster. For about two weeks, I practically stayed in the house and watched the news about the disaster that "Hurricane Katrina" caused. The category 5 storm flooded 80% of New Orleans, as a result there were over 1,800 dead.

It was sad to see how black people were being treated and how they were sleeping on their roofs for days waiting for F.E.M.A to recue them.

Minorities across the world protested that if it was white people instead of black, the government would've treated the situation differently.

On the anniversary of the 9/11 attack, I got a page from fat-boy.

When I called him I said, "What's up my nigga?"

He said, "ain't shit, yo, I'm a need you to come over the jungle and help come cook this food for the cook-out. I knew it wasn't going to be any cook-out. Fat-Boy wanted me to come over so I could cook some cocaine for him. Only time he ever called me to cook for him was when he had already fucked up the work, and needed me to fix it.

When I got over to Annie-May's apartment, fat-Boy had Cocaine and baking soda all over the kitchen counter top.

I said, "what up?"

"ain't shit", he replied.

I said, "what happened?"

He said, "I bought some oil base cocaine from a nigga up Baltimore and the shit lost a lot".

I said, "how much you cook up?"

He said, "a 8th"

I said, "how much baking soda you put in it?"

He said, "125 grams like you always taught me".

I said, "how much you get back?"

He said, "about 100 grams"

I picked the pyrex up and saw that it had a lot of oil base still in it.

I said, "the rest of your work is in the pyrex"

He said, "how can I get it out?"

I said, "I always told you that you can't cook all coke the same".

Fat-boy said, "I was used to cooking up that fish gail you were giving me, that's really the only way I know how to cook".

I said, "watch and observe".

I turned the stove on and sat the pyrex on the top of it. When the pyrex was hot enough, I poured some baking soda in my hand and started sprinkling it on top of the oil base. After all the Cocaine dropped to the bottom, I turned the water on in the sink and sprinkled cold water on the work so that the crack could get hard. After performing my magic trick by turning liquid into a solid, I took the crack out dropped it on some napkins to dry off.

When I put it on the scale it read 28 grams. I looked at Fat-Boy then said, "you didn't know that I knew magic did you?"

Fat-Boy was happy as shit.

He said, "thanks my nigga"

I said, "don't call me to cook no more coke up for you, because you know that I'm retired until another 4-5 months, consider that your last lesson until then".

He said "alright".

Annie-May walked into the kitchen and said, "ya'll see all them police outside?"

With a serious voice I said, "For real?"

Where Annie-May's apartment was, if you stood on the balcony, you could see the buildings parking lot.

When I opened the balcony door and stuck my head out, I saw about 20 police cars and about 50 officers walking around the building with K-9's. I immediately closed the door and said, "Fat-Boy, dump that shit, they bout to come up here!

I hurried up and got up out of Annie May's apartment because it was know telling what she had up in there. All the years that I've been in the game, I was never in a house raid.

When I got down to the building door, I heard my Cousin coming down the Stairs. Anni-May stuck her head out and yelled down the hallway, "ya'll didn't leave mine on the table, I said" shut the fuck up bitch! I walked out of the building and made a left towards the telephone booth.

"FREEZE . . . put your got damn hands in the air! When I looked up all I saw was Bossman and a whole police force full of guns pointing at me. While the K-9's barked repeatedly, I put my hands in the air then said, "what you fucking with me for now Bossman?"

He said, "I told you that your days were numbered. Now put your fucking hands behind your back".

Before I knew it, the whole neighborhood was outside looking at me getting handcuffed. Over the commotion of the crowd and the barking of the dogs, Fat-Boy yelled out, "What they locking you up for yo?"

I said, "I don't know . . . call Pack-O and tell him to come bail me out." You would've thought that I had just shot the President of the U.S. the way A.P.D. surrounded me and escorted me into the back of the police car.

Out of all the officers that were on the scene, I had to get taken down the police station by Bossman and his Flunky. When they got into the car, they both looked at me then started laughing.

I said, "What the fuck is so funny. I'll be back on the streets before the night is over." With his joker smile, Bossman pointed at the computer screen in the car and then said, "no you won't". When I lift-up in the back seat to get a closer look at the screen, it read "Federal Warrant". My heart felt like it stopped. I couldn't even move my lips to say anything, but that Federal Warrant word was tattooed in my mind.

It was a short ride to the station, all the shit they were talking, it was going in one ear and out the other. I was somewhat in shock, you would've thought that they had hit the million dollar lottery the way they was acting.

A paddy wagon pulled up and waited for me to enter in the back of it. I said, "where fuck I'm going at?" Bossman said, "your ass getting transported to the FEDS!!"

The Flunky said, "yeah . . . . I bet you won't be getting bailed out from them." The transporter was a black bald headed police officer who I'd never seen before. He walked to the back of the paddy wagon and opened the back door up.

While still laughing, the flunky helped me up the steps to the inside of the paddy wagon. Before closing the door Bossman said, "I'll see your ass in 10-20 years." I still could hear him and the flunky laughing while the paddy wagon drove off.

I thought about my mother and how she was going to feel when she got that phone call telling her that the FED's got her son. I could still remember what she said to me when I was in the hospital from my over dose, "I guess you going to keep getting arrested until you get the message."

Before we got on the highway, I looked out of the paddy wagon window for a couple of minutes. I stared at Naptown while it was literally faded away right before my eyes. I know that this was going to be the last time that I was going to see the Capitol of Maryland for a long time.

I guess it's true when they say, if a man keeps doing the same thing over and over and expects a different result, he's insane. While they both watched the paddy wagon drive away, Bossman said, "that niggers going to finally get what he deserves." The flunky smiled then said, "Who's next on the list boss?" Bossman inhaled, then let out a deep exhale and said, "Well son . . . I'm satisfied now . . . I think it's time for me to get my "Death with benefits." While looking surprised, the flunky looked at his Boss then said, "Your retiring?" Bossman looked at his protégé with his joker smile then said, "It's time for you to carry the torch now . . . always remember this . . . the best way to get rid of niggers is to take away their ability to reproduce themselves . . . so, make sure you hang as many of them niggers as you can." The flunky looked at his Boss and his hero then said, "I won't let you down."

Chapter 39

Game Over...

Nothing Is Ever Promised Tomorrow or Today

When I got out of the paddy wagon at Western District in Odenton, it was about 20 federal agents waiting for me. So many things were going through my mind at that time. I wondered was the rest of the family indicted also and if so, how many niggas underneath of them were coming for the ride. Who and how many houses the FED's hit and more importantly how much money and drugs did they get from the raids.

I wasn't worried about them hitting my townhouse because there wasn't anything illegal in there. One of the "rules" in the "Game" is that you never keep drugs or large amounts of money where you rest at. I knew that it was a good possibility that this day was coming, so I wasn't going to get caught sleeping. All my blood sweat and tears I put into the Drug Game wasn't going to go to waste. I probably wasn't going to enjoy my money, but my family would.

The paddy wagon driver guided me off the truck, took the handcuffs off of me, then handed me over to the "Big Boys."

The Federal agents stared at me like I was a terrorist that tried to blow up a Federal building. I guess to them I was the scum of the earth, but only God could judge me. The person in charge and who put the handcuffs on me was agent Thomas. After introducing himself he said, "do you know who we are?" I looked at his Mark Walberg ass, smirked then said, "ya'll the FED's . . . ain't ya'll?" Thomas said, "Me and about 10 agents here are D.E.A. and the rest are A.T.F." With a smart voice I said,

"Ok." Thomas said, "Let's go." He guided me inside the building into the interrogation room while his robots followed suit. He said, "have a seat." In the room was a desk, the chair I was sitting in and about 20 Federal agents all waiting for their turn to ask me questions.

Agent Thomas asked, "you want something to drink or anything else?" **Rule#1.** When your being interrogated, if they offer you anything "Don't take it." If you do take it, all it's going to do is make them want to question you more, because now they feel as though you owe them something. I heard so many so called "Gangsters" receive the offerings from the FED's and before you know it, they were taking an ink pen and telling on any and everybody they could think of. "Nawh, I'm good." I replied. Thomas said, "Mr. Walders ... or should I say 'Little Booh'?" I said, "You can call me whatever you want to because I'm not going to answer to either one." Thomas said, "Well little Booh, I want you to tell us about the bodies."

Rule#2. After they asked their first question, the only thing that should be coming out of your mouth is asking for a lawyer. If they continue to ask you questions, take a deep breath, relax yourself and try and think about some place happy. I said, "I want to talk to my lawyer." Thomas said, "We know you got white boy Mike killed ... Zeeto killed ... Stewy killed and got Grick shot." I had to laugh because I thought that they had me for a drug investigation. I knew that they didn't have any evidence on me for any murders. The other agents in the room whispered to each other while Thomas continued to ask his questions.

After about 15-20 minutes, I saw that Thomas and the other agents started getting frustrated, they knew that I wasn't going to do their job for them. I thought to myself, "Fuck they asking me questions for anyway, I thought the FED's were suppose to know everything." At that time, I thought this Federal shit was over rated. Everybody kept saying that the only thing that they fear is the FED's, fuck the FED's, they didn't know shit.

After about a half hour had passed, I broke my silence and said, "you mean to tell me that the Government can't spend money for F.E.M.A to help the victims of Hurricane Katrina, but they can spend money to come and lock my ass up?" Thomas once pale faced now turned red said, "get him the fuck up out of hear and take him to his cell! The A.T.F. agent named Flannigan, he had a familiar face, and he looked like a skinny version of Jack Black. He said, "let's go."

While walking to my cell I asked "how long am I going to be here?" He said, "tomorrow morning your going to 101 Lombard, that's a federal court building in Baltimore where a judge would decide to give you home confinement or keep you in custody until your trial date . . . yeah, you in the big leagues now."

I got no sleep in the cold cell. All I could think about is why this shit had to happen to me, shortly after I had stopped hustling. I guess it's true what they say, "as soon as you get your money right the FED's hit you with conspiracy."

When I did close my eyes, Flannigan banged on the cell door and said, "You ready?" When I lifted my head up from under my t-shirt, I looked somewhat surprised because I thought that I was dreaming. Flannigan popped my cell door and put the cuffs on me. While we walked to the entrance of Western District, agent Flannigan said, "You don't remember me do you?" I said, "Why should I?" He said, [At the Mike Tyson fight in D.C. . . . I was sitting right next to you and that pretty girl that was with you." I thought about it for a couple of seconds then said, "Oh-shit." He said, remember your girl friend took a picture of you and the Bishop Don Juan . . . I was the one that she asked could I take a picture of you and her." I said, "Damn, ya'll was on me like that?" He said, "We've been watching you for a while now."

❋ [While we waited at the entrance door, I heard a familiar voice coming from the back. I turned to the side and saw little-H and that nigga low with a dumb look on their faces. When I made eye contact with my cousin I whispered, "What the fuck going on?" He whispered back, "shit crazy." I didn't know what the fuck to think, my mind was puzzled. Here I am in Federal custody with these two dumb ass niggas.]

The ride to Baltimore was quiet and quick. It was September 12th, my 4 year anniversary from when I got released from the Maryland State System. I guess it's true what they say in Japan, the number 4 is bad luck.

I had a long 4 year run though, and I ran it like it was no tomorrow. I told niggas when I came home from up Jessup that they were going to feel it, and they did. Everybody and their mother in Naptown was going to remember the name 'Little Booh'. I made my mark in the Capitol of Maryland; any other hustler in my city would have to go through hell to try to top what I did. I was far from a Harvard student; I just had the balls to do it.

Yeah, that shit sounds good, but look at me now, on my way to a Federal arraignment. I guess in reality I grinded from the bottom just to make it to the bottom. I was hoping that I'll get house arrest until my trial date so that I could try and figure this shit out.

Chapter 40

101 Lombard

A t the court house I was guided to a booth where my lawyer was waiting for me. When I sat down in the chair, he asked, "how you doing?" I said, "How the fuck you think I'm doing?" He said, "I know things look bad . . . just hang in their . . . I talked to the Federal prosecutor this morning." I cut him off and said, "What they say I was locked-up for?" He pulled some papers out of his brief case then said, "this is your indictment." I grabbed it then said, "I know you already read it, so what did it say?" He said, "You got indicted by the FED's with individuals known as the 'Pioneer City Boys' for a police shooting and Conspiracy to sell cocaine." With a surprise look on my face I said, "What!!" The expression on my face told Larry that I couldn't believe that the Federalies indicted me with these charges. He said, "I didn't get a chance to comb through the indictment yet, but those are the charges that they are charging you with." I said, "What's up with the home confinement?" He said, "it's a 50/50 chance that you'll get it because your labeled as a major supplier in the indictment."

I said, "try to get that house arrest . . . I ain't trying to sit over the supermax until my trial date." Larry said, "I'm going to do my best." I said, "try harder." Larry said, "your mother and other family members are in the courtroom." Knowing that my family was in the courtroom supporting me, made me feel a little more relaxed." Larry said, "If you don't have anymore questions . . . I'll see you in the court room." I said, "Alright"

After about an hour had passed, a court Marshall came and put handcuffs on me and then escorted me to the elevator. I was shackled like a run away slave. On the 4ᵗʰ floor is where the Marshall guided me into the court room.

Everybody stared at me while I walked in. I locked eyes with my mother, letting her know that I was ok. I was seated next to "Little-H" and "Low" in the court room. We all were waiting to go through the same procedures.

The court appointed lawyers that "Little-H" and "Low" had looked as though they didn't have a clue what was going on with the case.

My lawyer's look was different, He was professional, and his name spoke for itself. I wanted to let the FED's know that I wasn't one of these nothing ass niggas that they were going to just do anything to. When I sat down, I looked back and saw my brother, sister, aunt and cousin looking at me like I was sitting in the electric chair.

It was about 10 federal agents in the room also, all who were looking at me and my co-defendants like we were prey and they were the predators.

＊[The prosecutor's name was Ms. Smithes. She was a Spanish woman with a nice built body and a nice size ass. If it wasn't for the job and the attitude, you could've easily mistaken her for a model with some sexy glasses on. When I made eye contact with her, she rolled her eyes and turned away. I had to come back to reality from fantasizing about fucking the prosecutor because this bitch was trying to hang me.

The bailiff hollered, "All rise!"

When the judge walked in the room, I studied her like the back of my hand. The look on her face told me that this bitch was out for justice, she wouldn't lose any sleep if she gave me a life sentence.

＊[Judge Baze had short jet black hair and she looked like an old miserable witch.

She said, "You all may have a seat."

Prosecutor said, "U.S. Government vs. Rome Walders." Larry tapped me on the shoulder so that I could stand up. After I stood, the prosecutor started to read all the charges that the Government had handed down to me. The stupid look that I had on my face was the same as when a deer is standing in front of head lights.

Larry whispered in my ear, "When the judge asks you how do you plea . . . tell her "Not Guilty." I gave him a fucked up look and with anger in my voice I said, "fuck I'm a plea guilty for . . . I didn't do any of that shit they charging me with?"

He said, "I'm going to get most of these dismissed, but its procedure that you plead not guilty to the charges on the indictment."

Judge Baze said, "How do you plea?" I said, "Not Guilty"

I looked back at my mother and saw the tears coming down her face. The judge kept talking but I wasn't paying attention to what she was saying. I felt bad because once again I've hurt my mother, this time seemed worse. When I came back to my senses, the Judge said, "Mr. Walders do you understand?"

I said, "Yeah." Without even knowing what I just agreed to.

Larry spoke up and said, "Your honor, I'm asking that my client be placed on Home Confinement until his trial date?"

The prosecutor jumped up then said, "Your honor . . . Mr. Walders is a major supplier in this indictment . . . so that makes him a flight risk and a danger to the community."

Larry said, "Your honor, my client has his mother here in the court today and she is more than willing to let him come to her house while on house arrest."

Ms. Smithen's said, "Your honor, Mr. Walders is a suspect in three murders . . . he's the type of person to get anything done at any given time."

Larry said, "my client hasn't been found guilty of these charges, so what the prosecutor is talking about is irrelevant."

The Judge stepped in and said, "Due to the fact that an officer has been shot in this investigation. I'm going to deny the request for Home Confinement for Mr. Walders."

After the Judge made her decision, my heart felt like it dropped. With no hesitation, Judge Baze said, "prosecutor, call your next case."

Chapter 41

Supermax Present

'Big-H' came to the Supermax about a month later; he got into a cell two doors down from me and his son.

All day and everyday while at the Max, he helped us dissect the indictment that the Government handed down to us.

'Big-H' was an expert in manipulating people into doing things for him. After only being at the max for a couple of months, he manages to convince the commissary worker to bring in two cell phones for me and his son. At that time I thought it was good money because the only people who I was calling was my mother and some females. I wasn't going to be dumb and talk business on the phone.

My lawyer came to see me the next week to share with me some information about the indictment. When I told 'Big-H' that I had a $75,000 lawyer, the way he acted you would've thought that he paid for it.

He said, "Why did you spend that much money on a lawyer when you could've used it for something else?"

I said, "Ain't no amount of money good enough for my freedom." He said, "You got to watch them lawyers ... because they all are working with the prosecutor." With a smart voice I said, "yeah-alright", then walked off the block to go to my attorney visit.

When I walked into the room, I saw Larry sitting there going through some papers.

He said, "how you doing Mr. Walders?" I said, "I'm doing ok considering my circumstances." After the C.O. shut the door I said, "You got some good news for me?" He said, "For starters ... anybody who is on your indictment that's mentioned but not charged, has cooperated with the FED's] Second, the attempted murder on the police officer charge, I got dropped because you weren't at the club when the officer got shot, and I also got carrying a firearm while being a convicted felon dismissed because you're not a convicted felon and there's no record of you having any kind of weapon in your possession."]

I said, "What about the conspiracy charge?" He said, "The FED's connected you with somebody in the 'Pioneer City Boys Gang.'"

[I said, "On the Overt Acts in the indictment, I was the only one that didn't get caught with anything . . . the FED's just got me labeled as a major supplier."]

Larry said, "Because there's about 10-15 people that went to the Grand Jury and testified that they bought drugs from you and that you're a major drug dealer."[I pointed at 'Big-H''s name then asked him, "Why is this person right here and me named as suppliers to this so called gang?"

He said, "Like I told you . . . anybody who's in your indictment and not charged has cooperated."]

*[Finding out that 'Big-H' had told on me, had me mad as shit. To myself I said, "All day long this nigga talking about snitches and he the main one telling. All I did was look out for his ass and this is how he repays me. No wonder he always wanted to use my phone so much, he probably was writing my #'s down and giving them to the FEDs'."

I came out of my zone when Larry said, "Mr. Walders, you ok?" I said, "Yeah . . . I'm good." He said, "You need to tell me something?" I pointed then said, ['that person[Anthony Howell] . . A.K.A. 'Big-H' who's mentioned but not charged in the indictment, is on the same tier with me right now." With a surprise look on his face he said, "You got to stay away from him . . . the FED's are more than likely trying to build more evidence against you." I said, "Don't worry about it . . . I'm two steps ahead of him."

He said, "Don't get yourself into any trouble while you're in here because it's going to look bad to the judge." I said, "What about another hearing on the house arrest?"

He said, "I think it's best that you stay in federal custody until your trial because it'll be easier for the FED's to gather more information on you if your back out in society." With anger in my voice I said, "I ain't trying to stay in this dirty as jail for a year."

He said, "I'm going to see what I can do about getting you transferred to one of the county's out on the Eastern Shore."

I said, "Alright ... try and make it close as possible to the Bay Bridge." He agreed and told me that he'll be back to see me next week. Before walking out the door he said, "Don't discuss your case with anybody and stay away from Anthony Howell." I said, "Alright"

When I got back to the block, the first voice that I heard was 'Big-H's'. He said, "little Booh ... what your lawyer talking about?"

I said, "My lawyer told me that anybody who was mentioned in the indictment but not charged has already cooperated with the Federal Authorities."

'Big-H' said, "I told you don't trust everything them lawyers say because they are lying and they give information back to the prosecutor." With a smart voice I said, "Why my lawyer got to lie to me ... What you think I paid $75,000 for?"

'Big-H' had guilt all over his face, 'Little-H' stood beside his father with a stupid look also. 'Big-H' tried to convince me that my lawyer was running some type of game on me but he knew my mind was made-up.

The first thing I did when I got into the cell was erase all the #'s I've been calling. It was all female's numbers anyway.

A week had passed and I'd been giving my cousin and his father the cold shoulder.

I ignored 'Big-H' because before this Federal indictment, he was considered a 'Soulja", now he was a rat. All his credibility and actions that once made people respect him went right out the window once he snitched and took that ink pen and wrote down statements for the Federal Agents, he wasn't a gangsta no more, now he was an off duty cop without the pension.

He use to have a firm grip now he dropped his name, shit was all good just a week ago.

'Little-H' got the cold shoulder because he still didn't realize that his father got him locked up just as-well, directly or indirectly.

The next morning, ugly ass Ms. Ray and about five other C.O.'s padded us down then started searching our cell. It was standard routine but this particular time I knew something didn't seem right.

The C.O.'s started opening up our commissary items like they was looking for something specific. 'Little-H' and I looked at each other with this stupid look on our faces. When Ms. Ray went to the cracker box, I put my head down and squinted my face because that was where my phone was. When she opened the box up, the cell phone fell out along with the adapter. Her ugly ass yelled out, "We got one cell phone!"

As she continued to search, she found 'Little-H''s phone under his pillow. She yelled out again, "We got another cell phone!" Ms. Ray stood in front of us with the two phones in her hand and said, "Who y'all get these from?" After a couple of seconds I said, "Them phones was in there when we first came into the cell."

With a smart look on her face she said, "Yeah right!" While we were being guided down the stairs by Ms. Ray and her clan, 'Big-H' yelled out, "Don't worry about nothing . . . I'm going to take care of everything." 'Little-H' said, "Alright" I said, "I bet you will."

We were guided to the other side of the Supermax, on the State side. It was used for high security inmates who didn't know how to act in the Maryland State System. The 23/1 lock-down, no visits and the hot ass cells kept the inmates yelling and selling death to each other all day and night.

When we got there, 'Little-H' and I were separated; I guess that was supposed to be a sign of punishment. The tier that I was put on was loud and smelled like shit.

When the C.O. walked me up the stairs to my appointed cell, it seemed like every inmate had their faces up against their cell windows looking at me.

Somebody yelled out, "What you in here for yo!"

"None of your fucking business" I replied back.

The C.O. yelled, "Open cell 18!"

When I got into my cell, I noticed that there wasn't any mattress on the concrete single bunk. With a smart voice the C.O. said, "You don't get any mattress when you on State Side lock-up . . . we ain't got money like the FED's." I gave him that same smart voice back and said, "What you say?" He yelled out, "Close cell 18!"

The 30 days I stayed on lock-up dragged on and on the 23/1 in a hot ass cell, no phone and one shower a week was enough to make a weak person go crazy. I was a 'Soulja' though, these obstacles were all part of being in the 'game'.

After about two months, 'Little-H' and I were taken off lock-up and sent back to F-Block. I was put into a cell on F-1 and Little-H' was put on F-3. I was ok with that because I didn't want to be around him or his father anyway.

The next day my lawyer came to see me at the Supermax. After greeting me Larry said, "Mr. Walders . . . I told you that you got to stay out of trouble while you are here." I played dumb and said, "What are you talking about?" He said, "The FED's got the cell phones and they're investigating them."

I said, "Them phones were in the cell when we first got there." Larry changed the subject and said, "I had a meeting with the prosecutor." I said, "Oh yeah? What she talking about?" He said, "She's asking that if you decide to cooperate about the murders, she could make this drug conspiracy go away."

With anger in my voice, I jumped up then said, "are you fucking crazy? . . . . I paid you all that money for you to tell me to snitch!" Larry's eyes widened-up, He must have thought he was going to get hit by me. He said, "NO!! . . . Mr. Walders you took that the wrong way." I said, "What fucking way was I suppose to have taken it?" He said, "As your lawyer it's my job to run by you all information pertaining to your case." I said, "You can tell that bitch that I don't know nothing about anything."

✳ [Larry said, "She also added that if you don't cooperate, then she is offering a plea of 7-9 years for the distribution of 2-3 and a half of kilo's of cocaine to the 'Pioneer City Boys' . . . the prosecutor knows that you had nothing to do with the police shooting so that's why the plea is what it is."]

I said, "Why the fuck am I pleading guilty to some kilo's that the FED's don't have any evidence on me about?" He said, "She gave you a week to make your decision." I said, "You think she's bluffing?"

Larry said, "Mr. Walders you hired me to be your lawyer. If you decide that you want to go to trial then I'm prepared or if you decide to take the plea, it's your decision to make but if you're found guilty you're looking at 15-20 years." I was puzzled; I didn't want to make the wrong decision because I had no type of knowledge with the Federal law. I said, "Come back and see me in a couple of days . . . I'll have my decision then."

Before leaving, Larry said, "You're going to have to start trusting me." With a smirk on my face I said, "Yeah-right"

✳ Back at my cell, I thought long and hard about what Larry had told me. [My cell buddy was a Yankee named 'Bishop" who came to Baltimore the year before because him and a couple of his men heard that the dope money was good in the city. After only being in Baltimore for about a month, two of his men got killed and the FED's snatched him up for having a gun in his possession. All I could say to him was "got to B-more careful."

Bishop said, "Yo-B . . . I think you should take the plea."

I said, "I ain't going to do 7-9 years for some shit that they don't have any evidence on me." He said, "Think about it B, if you go to trial, the jury's going to find you guilty because evidence or not ... all them niggas going to come to court and testify against you anyway ... why do them rat ass niggas a favor and go to trial, and after they finish telling on you, they get another downward departure off of their sentence."

That did make since though, I definitely didn't want them bitch ass niggas benefiting anymore off of me.

That whole night, I laid on my bunk and thought long and hard about my situation. I got away with a lot of criminal acts in my life time, I guess this was punishment for it and it was going to be up to me how this was going to play out.

Later the next day, Bishop asked me, "You made your decisions B?" I said, "I'm a take the plea." He said, "Smart move" I said, "This the price I'm a have to pay for all the other shit I got away with in my life." He said, "Don't forget to tell your lawyer to make sure that safety valve and known and unknown is on your plea." That's so that the FED's can't come back later in the future and supersede you. Anything except for murders because the statute of limitations never expires on that act ... you know niggas get locked-up everyday, it won't take nothing for them to tell on you about some other shit. These mother fucking FED's don't play fair -B, for example, whatever type of drugs they confiscate off of a person they say that over the years of you being investigated that it was 50 times the actual proof ... Even worse, with conspiracy the feds don't need any proof, just one or two people.

After informing Larry that I was taking the plea, I was packed up and down Tailbot county the next day. Lil H came down about a month later. Tailbot county detention center was a clean jail and the small town reminded you of Mayberry. The disadvantage was that the federal inmates were mixed in with the local inmates. Some of them might get a bail as low as $50 and couldn't get out, but the federal inmates had no bail, which kept tension in the air. "Across the bridge niggas", is what they called us. As soon as I got on the tier the first person I saw was "Clown", he was an O.G. who got locked up for manufacturing cocaine on Cheek-o's case. The next person I saw was Blew from up Freetown.

✳ Something wasn't right. On the Advert Acts in our indictment, it specifically said that 'Little H' sold 14 grams of crack cocaine base, so how he sign for 5 grams instead of 14 grams of crack.

Every time someone came to Talbot County from the Supermax, they said it was rumored that 'Big H' and 'Little H' both were "hot" ["Big-H" had been going in and out of the Max to profit hearings (cooperating), and 'Little H' is suppose to be scheduled to testify in court on 40-cal for shooting the police officer. ["Goody" and his brother 'H' was two of the biggest drug dealers that came out of West Baltimore. When they both came to the jail, they "co-signed" that the rumors were true.]

The months at Talbot dragged on and on. I had completely cut 'Little H' off because now I had concrete proof that he was a rat. Like father, like son, huh?

'Little H' made his choice to sell drugs, nobody put a gun to his head and made him do it. Now he was trying to cheat his way through life.

If you commit suicide, lie to get something that you want or snitch on someone to benefit yourself, it all comes back on you. You can't cheat your way through life, the best thing you should do is 'man-up'.

You only get one life because it's not a sequel, pussy ass niggas treat life like it's a rehearsal. [First they snitch on you, then try to live as though it never happened, like they got 9 lives and shit.]

The time that I've spent down in Talbot County, I found peace with myself. In a crazy way, I was somewhat ok with being locked-up. I didn't have to worry about niggas trying to murder me or putting my family in any danger. I slept a lot easier at night. The part about me being watched by APD, FED's investigators and don't forget about the haters, was enough to drive a sane person crazy. When you get tired of running from the pain, the only thing left to do is to face it.

✱[Blew was leaving the next day to go back to the Supermax because his trial was in a couple of weeks. [He informed me that he was going to Claim Salvent, live flesh and blood, U.C.C.(Uniform commercial code). In a nut shell, federal inmates were letting the Government know that they had no authority to charge them. Which is true because the constitution clearly explains that the Government can only charge crimes that are on federal property and corporate companies, anything else was the state's problem. This routine had the federal courts backed-up because the inmates refused to go through all of the court procedures. Any legal mail that was sent to them was not signed because they refused to sign any mail that the Government capitalized the letters to make an inmate a corporation, and if you signed it, then your agreeing with them. Almost every inmate that came to Supermax was asked to join the U.C.C. I wasn't going to do that procedure though, I just wanted to get the fuck out of the FED's way.

✱ "Blew" and I became cool with one another during our stay at Talbot County. A couple of months later, "Clown" had left to go back to the Max so that he could prepare for his sentence.

The FED's weren't playing with niggas, the basketball numbers they were giving out got inmates mind right.

It was the end of the summer when I had gotten a letter from my lawyer. He informed me that all my co-defendants had cooperated and were scheduled to go to court in November to testify against 40-cal for the attempted murder on the police officer.

All my co-dee's grew-up with "40-cal". Since they were young and now they were all ready to testify against him like it was nothing.

My birthday had come and gone and just like it was scheduled, 'Little H' was packed up and on his way back to the Supermax. When I saw him walking down the hallway, I yelled out, "Where you going at?" Like I didn't already know, I just wanted to let him know that I knew he was about to testify on "40-cal". He said, "I'm on the way back to the supermax because I'm going to court next month for sentencing!" With a smart voice I said, "Do the right thing!" He just walked off without saying anything else.

✱ The day after "40-cal" went to court, I called "Black" up to see what was the outcome. I said, "What's up my nigga?" He said, "Ain't shit . . . how you holding up?" I said, "same ol' same ol'" He said, "I was at Moon's barber shop this morning and "40-cal's" people were in there . . . they said that "40-cal" got found guilty and that he was going to get a mandatory life sentence." ✱

I said, "Damn!" He said, "That nigga 'Low' got on the stand and admitted that he had been a federal informant since the year 2001. He talked about how he saw 40-cal shoot the officer then witness him urinate on his hand to try and wash off the gun powder." I said, "I knew that nigga was a rat." "Black" said, "The nigga 'Fab-O' was on the stand for an hour and half, niggas say that he talked so much that the prosecutor had to give him some water because his mouth was so dry."

We both gave out a little Hyena laugh, then I yelled, "Rat bastard". He said, "Little-H ain't no different from them niggas, he's a piece of shit also."

I said, "What that nigga say when he testified?" Black said, "After he told on 40-cal he told the prosecutor that he was buying drugs from his cousin 'Little Booh' down in Annapolis and that you're a major supplier of the 'Pioneer City Boys'." I said, "What!" Black said, "Oh yeah . . . Fab-O also said that he was buying drugs from you." I said, "I ain't surprised about them snitch ass niggas. It was in their blood since their mother's boar them . . . but I am however surprised that 'Little H' would even speak my name in vain."

✷ [Black also informed me that a lot of people were saying that the investigation was really on the nigga "Los", but after he got slumped they used me as a substitute to complete their indictment.]

After I got off of the phone, I went back to my cell and thought about how the FED's could turn a weak person suicidal in no time.

This technique that the FED's use to turn blacks against blacks goes way back to the "Willie Lynch Theory" (The making of a slave).

✦[Willie Lynch was a British slave owner in the West Indies. He was invited to give a speech at the colony of Virginia in 1712 to teach his method to slave owners there. The term "Lynching" is derived from his last name.

In his letter among many other things he ensured the slave owners that he had a full proof method to controlling their slaves for at least 300 years. On the top of his list was 'Age', but the only reason it was at the top of the list was because it starts with the letter 'A'. He explained how important it was to turn the old slave against the younger slave, and the younger slave against the older slave. Second was 'color' or shade. He explained how important it was to turn the light skin against the dark skin slave and the dark skin slave against the light skin slave.

✦[The Willie Lynch Theory still lives on to this day. Black people are the most racist people on the planet! 93% of the murders in this country are black on black crimes. If your black and not from one of the well known states, you're going to be disliked by other blacks in any Penal or Federal system. Even if you're from a well known state but you're not from a certain city in that state, you're disliked. Even if you're from a well known city in that state but not from a certain block, you're going to be disliked too. Inmates in the Federal system call it "Set tripping"]

In the African American male culture, if you're light skin, your labeled as being a "Pretty ass Nigga". If you're dark skin, your labeled as a "Black ass nigga."

In the African American female culture, if you're light skin, you're labeled as having Indian in you because of the texture of your hair. If your dark skin, you're labeled as wearing a weave, kinky or untamed hair.

Ask yourself, when was the last time that you've seen a dark completion woman win a 'Beauty Pageant' contest or the 'Next Top Model'.

It's also being shown on B.E.T. (Black Entertainment Television). Look at your normal rap videos, 90% of the females that are chosen to be featured in these videos are light complexion or of a different race. It's no secret that rap artist are fascinated by foreign felions.

In the street life, the FED's were the slave master because they could clearly do whatever they wanted to do with the minority. They'll get the young Hustlers to tell on the old Hustlers, the old hustlers to tell on the young hustlers and anything in between.

The Federal and Penal prisons today are nothing but modern day slave plantations. Black and Latinos are being locked-up and sent to prison to work for as little as 19 cents a day. The cycle continues when a son grows up without a father only to look to the streets for answers. A daughter becomes a "black girl" lost, stripping in a club or prostituting her body because no father figure was around to teach her how to respect herself.

When Abraham Lincoln first signed the papers to free the slaves, that was the same day that white folks started to build the first jail. The racist Americans put his face on a brown coin and made it worth the least among our currency. That was Lincoln's punishment for turning his back on White America.

We as black people are the minority; we are only 13% of the United States population. It's a "conspiracy" that we're more than half of the population in the prison systems. It's no secret that we aren't meant to survive because it's a set up. We as the minority don't own any airplanes or boats, so how is it that the drugs and guns just so happened to end up in our communities. In addition, the liquor stores on ever corner just add fuel to the fire. 70% of murders in the country are made by a person under the influence of drugs or alcohol.

The next day I got legal mail from my lawyer informing me that I had a court date for the up coming month to be sentenced. Go figure! I guess the prosecutor wanted my co-dees to say on court record that I was a major supplier of their gang, just in case I decided to say "Fuck the plea" and go to trial at the last minute.

I was glad to have finally gotten a court date so that I could get this shit over with.

Later that day, I took some scissors and cut my dreads off. I've made up my mind that I wasn't going to go to sentencing with dreadlocks down past my shoulders, looking like a menace to society. I figured, if I go to court with a low cut, the judge might look at me as being a little child that made a mistake in his life.

Two weeks later, I was packed up and on my way back to D.O.C.

Chapter 42

American Justice

BANG, BANG, BANG . . . Walders!!!
4:30 a.m., Ms. Barrocks ugly ass banged on my cell door.

I yelled out, "Yeah"

She said, "Walders . . . get your ass up, you got court this morning!"

All my property had been packed since the night before. I couldn't wait to get to 101 Lombard and this situation over with. Ever since I stepped foot back in Baltimore City, the butterflies had been eaten at my stomach from wondering how Judge Dave was going to act with my plea.

My cell buddy was from out Cecil County, a white boy named Josh. He said, "Make sure you get that safety valve on your plea?" I said, "I'm definitely not going to forget about that."

When I got over to the court house, I was informed by inmates in the bullpen that Josh was hot. He was suppose to have told on somebody from Philly in exchange, the FED's wouldn't charge his mother on his indictment. The whole time in the cell at D.O.C., Josh had convinced me that people were telling on him. The FED's were crazy like that, a rat could be right underneath your nose and you wouldn't even know it.

Fifteen of us crowded up in the bullpen and we all sat curious, anxious and nervous at the same time, knowing that our life was in the hands of the Judge. We all had been kidnapped by the Government. And now were waiting for the abuse that was promised to us.

Before the marshal took me upstairs to the court room, I was placed in a booth where my lawyer was waiting to see me.

After greeting me as usual, Larry said, "Howell Jr. got sentenced to 6 ½ years yesterday and your other co-defendants didn't get sentenced yet."

To myself I thought, "Damn . . . Little H testified on his man and still got Federal time . . . The FED's don't give a fuck about a snitch, they'll send you in the same system with the same person you testified on."

That 6 ½ years Little H got, going to seem like 50 years to him. Imagine him doing his sentence while being labeled as a rat. Even when he get home, "he'll always be in jail just minus the bars".

⌈My co-dee's got a lifetime scar that even the world's best plastic surgeon with a horse shoe up his ass couldn't hide. All them niggas were hotter than the sun dipped in black. They can avoid the cage, but they can't avoid the grave.⌋

Larry brought me back to reality when he said, "When the Judge ask do you have anything to say, show remorse and keep it short and sweet."

I said, "I ain't gonna say nothing stupid . . . I'm going to accept responsibility for my actions and that's it. Even though the only evidence that the FED's have on me is the "Boca Raton".

Larry said, "What does that word mean?"

I said, "It means the mouth of the rat." He gave out a little laugh then said, "I didn't know that,". But I wasn't laughing because in a couple of minutes Judge Dave was gonna decide my future. Larry asked, "Do you have any questions for me?" I said, "Fight hard for that seven years." He said, "I'll do my best."

Before leaving he told me to be strong and keep my head up.

After a couple of minutes the Marshall opened the door cuffed me up and then guided me to the elevator. When we got off, the butterflies started to eat at my stomach and my heart pounded violently in my chest.

When we walked in the court room through the back door, everybody got quiet. They all looked at me as if I was walking to my execution chair.

It looked as though the Marshall was walking me in slow motion so that everybody could get a good look at me. Even if I wanted to, I couldn't move any faster because my ankles were shackled together. I was chained up like a runaway slave that had just gotten captured.

I continued to hold my head up high because I had nothing to be ashamed of, I played with the cards I was given. Even though I knew life had dealt me a bad hand, I still tried to make some good come out of it.

The first face I recognized was my mother's, she was towards the back of the court room sitting in the first row. I gave her a smile hoping that it would let her know that I was going to be ok

When I got to my chair, Larry greeted me with a pat on my back. After the Marshall took the hand cuffs off me, Larry whispered to me, "The prosecutor says that she'll make no argument about you getting sentenced to the seven years." I said, "good". I looked over at Ms. Smithens and observed how phat her ass looked in that dress she had on. Larry brought me back to reality by telling me to have a seat.

After I sat down, I looked at all the faces that shared the court room with me. Black, Meeka, my aunt and my cousin Tonya were all seated in the first row next to my mother. Bossman and his flunky were seated next to agent Thomas in a section towards my left with about 10 other agents. I know Bossman and his protégé weren't going to pass up this opportunity to see me at my worst. When Bossman and I made eye contact, he gave me a smile; I gave him one right back. I wasn't going to let him or any of these federal mother fucker's see me hurt.

The bailiff yelled "All rise!"

Judge Dave walked in and glanced at me with a serious look on his face while he proceeded to his bench.

After sitting down he said, "You may be seated"

Ms. Smithens said, "Your honor … we are here today for case #5321.6 United States vs. Rome Walders".

Judge Dave said, "You may proceed."

My lawyer said, "Your honor … I'm Larry Natans representing Rome Walders in this case". Judge said, "Mr. Natans . . . your client pleaded guilty to distribute 2-3 and a half kilo's of cocaine?" Larry said, "Yes your honor". Judge said, "Ms. Smithens you may inform me on the facts in this indictment".

The prosecutor went on and on how I was supposedly the main supplier of the 'Pioneer City Boys', and that is if this case would've gone to trial she had a number of people that were willing to come to court and testify against me. After she finished, Judge Dave said, "Mr. Natans you want to add anything?"

Larry said, "Your honor … the prosecutor and I agreed that my client should get the lower end of the plea because he wasn't involved in the police shooting which is the main situation in this indictment."

Ms. Smithens said, "That's true your honor". Judge said, "Is there anybody in the court room who wants to speak on Mr. Walders behalf?"

My mother stood and said, "Yes your honor"

When I looked and saw my mother walking forward, I noticed how red her eyes were from crying. She said, "I'm Joan Hix, mother of Rome Walders." Judge said, "You can continue"

Between the tears my mother said, "My son is a good person, of course he made some mistakes, but what child hasn't. I raised two boys practically by myself in drug infested neighborhoods. I provided for them the best way I could. Your honor, if you give my son another chance at life, I'm sure that he'll do better."

I got teary eyed seeing my mother crying and practically begging this judge to spare my life. I couldn't see the tears coming down my eyes because Bossman and his protégé and all the other agents would've loved to see a sign of weakness from me. That wasn't going to happen because I had the heart of a Lion.

After my mother finished Judge Dave said, "Thank you Ms. Hix ... Mr. Walders do you have anything to say before I announce your sentence?" I stood in front of the Judge with no honor, because I didn't agree with my charges, looked him in the eyes and said, "Judge Dave . . . I accept responsibility for my actions and if your willing . . . I just want to be able to make it back to society so that I could start doing the right thing . . . Thank you."

Larry said, "Your honor, Mr. Walders graduated from high school and planned on going to college before this situation occurred."

Judge Dave said, "Mr. Walders . . . I'm going to sentence you to 96 months in a federal prison along with 5 years probation upon your release for your roll in the indictment." The look on my face was a mixture of anger and shock because the judge didn't give me the low end of my plea.

Larry said, "Your honor, the prosecutor and I agreed on the low end."

Judge said, "I think he deserves the 96 months for being a major supplier in this case . . . along with a $100 court fee . . . I also read in your PSI(Pre-sentence investigation) that you have overdosed on crack cocaine, so I'm going to recommend the drug program."

Larry said, "Your honor, my client would like to be sent to a prison that's close to Baltimore." Judge said, "I'll recommend that."

When I looked back at my family, I observed them counting on their fingers trying to figure out how many years was 96 months. I looked at my mother, gave her a smile and whispered to her that I had gotten 8 years. She gave me a smile back letting me know that as long as I was ok with it, she was ok with it.

I thought back when I first started to hustle, the main reason was to help my mother out from struggling, but ever since I'd gotten involved with drugs, all I did was cause my mother more hurt than anything.

The catch to my sentence is that I really got 13 years because if I go back out into society and violated my probation, Judge Dave can sentence me the whole 5 years. It was crazy because even after you do your time in prison, the FED's still kept a rope around your neck hoping you'll hang yourself.

Meeka whipped her eyes and whispered for me to call when I can. Black gave me a serious head nod letting me know that he was going to hold shit down for me while I was gone. My cousin and aunt just stared at me.

Judge Dave stood up from his thrown then walked out of the court room. I guess with the job he has, he was tired of seeing young black males coming in his court room.

When the Marshall put the shackles back on me, I looked back at my family one last time and told them that I loved them.

While walking pass Bossman and the rest of the officers of the law, I gave them all a smile with a nod of my head. The smile was to let them know that the 8 years wasn't nothing to me, it was all part of being in the game. It cost to be the Boss, so I guess it's time for me to pay my debt to society once again. The nod was to remind them that they didn't get any money from me. The little over seven figures that I had hidden was going to keep me motivated and focused to do this time and not let the time do me. "The fastest way to start the longest journey is a single step."

I was guided back to the attorney booth where I was informed that my lawyer wanted to talk to me.

I wasn't upset with Larry, because I knew he had done his best, but I also knew that the judge had the final decision.

Larry walked in, the look on his face showed that he was sad of the judge's decision. He said, "I'm sorry things didn't turn out the way we wanted it to." I said, "You don't have anything to be sorry about . . . you tried." He said, "I talked to your family to make sure that they understood what went on."

I asked, "How they doing?"

He said, "Your mother says that she's going to be ok and the same for the rest of your supporters here today. I told them that you'll be transferred to Ohio until the BOP (Bureau of Prison) calculates your security level. If you need anything call me collect."

I said, "Alright"

Before leaving he said, "Keep your head up and don't worry about the court fee, I'll take care of it."

Back at D.O.C., I was put in a cell with a nigga that just the day before got a life sentence. His name was "Rob" and he was from over West Baltimore. He was alright though; Rob was taking the life sentence like a Soulja. All that night he talked about how he got a good chance to appeal his case because the evidence against him was weak. I went to sleep on him though because I had my own problems to deal with.

I was awakened the next morning by Ms. Barrocks banging at the cell door. She said, "Walders" I said, "Yeah", she said, "Pack up everything . . . you getting transferred to Ohio." I said, "Damn . . . these mother fucka's didn't waste no time getting me up out of D.O.C.".

Rob asked, "Did that bitch say my name yo?"

I said, "Nawh"

He said, "I'm ready to get the fuck up outta here."

I said, "This 23/1 D.O.C. lock down shit is crazy . . . you don't even get fresh air here."

Ms. Barrocks came back about an hour later, opened the cell door and said, "C'mon Walders". Rob said, "Ms. Barrocks . . . my name ain't on the transfer list?" With a smart voice she said, "Did I call your name?"

Rob said, "You ain't gotta get fucking smart . . . that's why you look like mighty Joe young's sister . . . your ugly bitch!"

Ms. Barrocks just sat outside of the cell door and took the verbal abuse that Rob had given her. I gave out a little Hyena laugh, while walking out the cell I said, "Rob keep your head up" He said, "Alright" When I walked out the cell, Ms. Barrocks closed the door then yelled, "That's why you got life mother fucka!" I said to myself, "That bitch would say that disrespectful shit after she closed the door."

Rob yelled, "Bitch when I come out for breakfast, I'm going to piss and shit your ass down"

While Ms. Barrocks guided me to the elevator, she just laughed and laughed.

Me and four other federal inmates rode on the transportation van, on our way to 101 Lombard. We all sat quietly while looking out of the window because we knew that this was going to be the last time that we'd see Baltimore for awhile.

At the court house, Ohio Marshalls strip searched us one by one, shackled us, then gave us a jump suit. The 5 ½ hour ride seemed like a 10 hour journey

If somebody would've asked me, "Do to the situation I was in, would I have not played the game and joined the army?" I would have said, "HELL NAWH".

What I look like going to another country and fighting a war that has nothing to do with me or my family . . . I'd rather do 8 years in a federal prison any day than to go in the army . . . "Join the army and be all you can be", don't that sound like some dumb shit.

Society only gave people that were the same color, and grew up in the same environment as me one game to play. The Fed's ain't play fair though. They'd turn weak niggas into rats, coach them, then use them as mouth pieces to make statements. The Boca-Raton never hesitated to give information about the underworld that was once protected by the code of the streets.

Ohio just had a blizzard a couple of days ago, so the whole Youngstown was covered with snow. The privately owned Institution's job was to detain and get inmates prepared for prison.

The Federal inmates from Youngstown who were awaiting court dates wore yellow, while the other inmates who were already sentenced wore orange. Altercations occurred between the two colors constantly. The cafeteria was labeled as being the battle ground because the dorms and the rec. yard kept the two colors segregated.

Ohio was so packed that two men cells were turned to three, the only thing that was added was a tub and a mattress.

After being stripped searched by the C.O., I was placed in cell block A-07. There were about 15 tiers in the facility that held 180 Federal inmates each. I had two cell buddies, one was a Yankee and the other from V.A. Tony was a Spanish nigga from Brooklyn that thought he was the slickest person that came out of the rotten apple. Bobby was a white boy from Alexandria, VA that smelled like dumpster juice.

After introducing ourselves to one another, they put me down with some helpful information about how the Federal system works. Tony said, "B . . . you gonna be here 3 weeks to a couple of months". I said, "Damn . . . why that long?" Bobby said, "After the B.O.P. calculate your security level, then they're going to designate you to a prison."

Tony said, "How many points you got B?" I said, "More than likely . . . I'll be going to a low security prison . . . at the worst, a medium." Tony said, "After you leave here, you going to the air lift" ⌐

I asked, "What's that?" Bobby said, "That's where everybody goes before they go to their designated prison." Tony said, "Hopefully you don't have to get on the air plane -B . . . Hopefully you'll get sent to a prison close to home."

On the tier, there were four T.V.'s in the rec. area, in order to listen to them you'd need an institutional walkman radio.

There were four phones, the only way you could use them is with an institutional phone card.

It was a fairly clean facility; the only thing that was filthy was the six showers. They all looked and smelled like a country out house.

The rec. yard had two basketball whole courts in the middle of the yards track. It made no since that they would have two phones outside by the basketball courts because you couldn't hear over the loud inmates.

The federal inmates that were in the institution were from all over the United States. The FED's have supposedly taken the most dangerous people in America, no matter their race or gang they ran with and put them all in one big building in Ohio. You had to be cautious when you in a situation like this, because tension stayed in the air 24/7. Stabbings, assaults and other violent acts occurred regularly during the course of the day. After every incident, the staff would only lock us down just long enough to get the blood cleaned up.

The counselor came on the tier and gave me an institutional walkman for the T.V., a calling card for the phone, and my ID #.

Your last three digits on your I.D. # was very important in the FED's. Since my case was in Maryland, my last three numbers were 037. It didn't matter where you were from, if your case was in Maryland your last digits were 037.

I called my mother to let her and the rest of my family know that I was ok. The 10 minute phone call went so fast and it was $9 a clip.

I was at Ohio for 2 and half weeks when the counselor let me know that I was on the transfer list. I was glad that I was designated so quickly because between Tony talking too much about nothing and Bobby snoring, I was ready for the federal system. They both had been waiting to get transferred for about a month, they were upset that their name wasn't on the list.

The day after Christmas, I was packed up and was on a big blue bus with 39 other inmates on our way to the Air lift.

The 7 and half hour ride to Harrisburg had my ass numb from bouncing up and down on the medal seats, every time we hit a bump. It also didn't help that the bathroom in the back had the bus smelling like shit and piss mixed.

The Air lift's scenery was just like on the movie 'Con-Air'. The twenty bus loads filled with inmates, lined up side by side, all watched as the air planes landed. Over a hundred Marshalls with automatic firearms watched over the area to make sure that the exchanges of inmates were complete without interference. When I saw all those marshals at one time, I knew that the FED's were serious.

The butterflies started to upset my stomach as soon as I saw the first plane land. Just the thought of me being shackled on an air plane made me want to throw up.

The FED's had the power to send you to any prison in the United States of America.

We all watched the inmates as they departed off of the air planes, all of them looked beat up and battered. I guess the turbulence and fear of the plane crashing got the best of them.

Everybody on the bus was quiet while the marshals read the names of the inmates who were getting on the air planes to go only god knows where. Due to the B.O.P. policy and security reasons, an inmate couldn't be informed on what prison he/she were getting transferred to.

A half hour later, my name was called. When I walked off of the bus, the only thing that was going through my mind was being shackled on an air plane. Five marshals waited for me outside, they all had the look on their faces that said, "I wish you would run so that I can put a bullet in your head."

After taking my shoes off and opening up my mouth like they ordered me to, I was guided four buses over. I was happy as shit to be going the opposite direction of the air planes. The butterflies that once upset my stomach disappeared instantly.

The bus was packed, soon as I step foot on it, I could feel the tension. The look on our faces showed anger from the Government kidnapping us, and now we're being transported to a plantation to become slaves. We all were chapters of the same book, but just from a different page.

I finally found a seat in the back by the bathroom. When I sat down, I glanced at the person next to me so that I could size him up just incase he start to act up during the bus ride.

Besides the funky bathroom, the soft seats ensured me a comfortable ride to whatever prison I was going to.

About 10 minutes into the ride, the person next to me asked, "Where you coming from -B?" When he called me -B, I knew he was a Yankee. "Ohio", I replied. He said, "I'm Bum" I said, "I'm Booh"

The nigga looked just like Michael Jordan with braids in his hair. I asked him, "where this bus going at?" He said, "We going to Pennsylvania". I said, "That's what's up." I really didn't care where I was going, as long as I really wasn't on that air plane.

Bum said, "We going to Lewisburg Penitentiary for a hold over . . . then tomorrow we'll be going to our designated prison."

I said, "Oh alright" . . . I thought you were going to say that we were staying at Lewisburg." He said, "You ain't got penitentiary points do you?" I said, "Nawh . . . the highest security level I'm going is a medium." He said, "Yeah . . . you'll be back on the bus tomorrow morning."

I remember seeing Lewisburg Penitentiary on the history channel when I was at home. The correspondent talked about how after the riots kicked off in '98, the guards were under investigation for bringing real knives in the prison and giving them to the A.B.(ARION BrotherHood). Three African Americans from D.C. got killed in that riot. As time went on, the case against the guards seemed to have vanished.

Chapter 43

The Penitentiary-Adapt or Die

I slept practically the whole four and half hour ride to Lewisburg, Pennsylvania. When I woke up we were at the prison.

Lewisburg Penitentiary looked like an old Castle, it was built in the 1930's and looked every bit of it.

After the guard in the tower approved they opened the gate for us, we slowly moved closer to the prison. Even though it was dark, the lights that surrounded the prison shinned the area up like it was a bright sunny day.

When the bus stopped, the door opened up and a man entered. He introduced himself as Lieutenant Johnson. By the look of the gray hair and the black rings under his eyes, you could tell that the old penitentiary had done damage to him.

He said, "When y'all hear your name ... step to the front of the bus."

With his Pennsylvania accent, no colored person on that bus would've argued that he was a 'Klu Klux Klan' member.

All of us sat quietly while waiting for our name to be called by the Grand Wizard. After a couple of minutes, my name was called and I walked to the front of the bus. Lieutenant Johnson signaled me to proceed outside of the bus where one of his C.O.'s waited for me.

He said, "Down the stairs"

The cold Pennsylvania winter air distracted me as I glanced at him and then continued my journey to the entrance of the castle.

They put all 40 of us into a room where the C.O.'s un-shackled us, and waited on Lieutenant Johnson to come to give them further instructions.

After a couple of minutes, Johnson walked in, stood at the door way and just stared at us. The scenery was like at a slave auction and Lieutenant Johnson was studying us to make his bid.

He yelled, "Y'all listen up . . . I'm a call out some names . . . if your name is called, step forward!"

After the Grand Wizard called out six names, he called mine. I thought it was just standard routine. When I stepped towards Johnson, he signaled me to go down the hall to the bullpen.

About twenty yards down the hallway, I walked into the funky ass bullpen. The toilet had shit and old piss still in it, the smell had my stomach doing summer salts. One of the niggas that shared the bullpen with me tried to flush it, but it wouldn't cooperate. About fifteen minutes later, Johnson walked in and said "Y'all get use to seeing my face . . . because y'all are designated here at Lewisburg."

At the moment, my eyes widened up and I thought to myself, "How the fuck I'm designated here." Not being afraid, but being in shock to having penitentiary points.

Johnson said, "Y'all going to follow me down the hall to where my staff is, and that is where y'all going to be strip searched for any contraband."

The only thing that was going through my mind was that it had to be a mistake. Anybody in their right mind who was entering a place like this for the first time, had no choice but to wonder what was waiting for them behind the haunted doors.

When we got to the other end of the hallway, it was seven C.O.'s who took us all through the regular routine. We were told to strip ass naked, bend over, spread our ass cheeks, lift up our feet, and then open our mouths. That's one thing that I could never get use to, any grown man would've felt violated by letting another man look at him naked.

After getting my Lewisburg package and putting my uniform on, I quickly got over the violation because I had bigger fish to fry.

Lieutenant Johnson and his Klansmen guided us up stairs to the S.H.U. (Special Housing Unit), that's what lock up was called up Lewisburg. You could hear the inmates that shard the S.H.U. holler on all three floors.

When we got to the top floor, Johnson said, "Y'all going to be in the S.H.U. for 1-2 weeks until y'all go to 'Qaid' . . . that's where y'all going to be interviewed to see if it's ok for y'all to go out to the compound.

While walking down the hallway to my cell, I could feel the tension in the air. Niggas had their faces pressed up against their cell doors trying to get a good look at the fresh blood.

I was put in a cell with this crazy person that just came from "Big Sandy", which was another killing field penitentiary, but it was in Texas.

All my cell buddy did was sit on the floor and talk to himself all night long. Soon as I stepped foot in the cell, I sized his ass up. I didn't get any sleep that first night. I kept my shoes on and the institution pen that was given to me in my Lewisburg package, stayed in my hand, just in case this nigga decide to act up.

The next day, I went outside in the small cage to get some fresh air. I observed how inmates walked the track in the yard, while some worked-out on the weight pile.

Lewisburg had a big ass yard. Besides exercising the criminal mind, a lot of inmates occupied their time by participating in the activities that the penitentiary allowed them to do.

Inmates in the cage that shared the S.H.U. with me, hollered onto the yard at their comrades to send messages or give "green lights" to ok assaults on other inmates.

A lot of love ones get it twisted because they think every jail or prison is the penitentiary, that's not true.

In the State system you got about six different security levels. Maximum security and higher are considered the penitentiary, anything underneath that is a less secured level.

Each state labels all its federal penitentiary's, and to make it official, they surround the prison with a big ass wall which nobody can see in it, and you can't see out of it.

Nothing or nobody in this world could've prepared me for a federal penitentiary, but I can adapt to any type of environment being the person I was. I carried it the same way I carried it on the streets', "A no tolerance rule". I was always humble, but never taken advantage of.

The federal prison is way different from the Maryland State system. In my state, you'll have about 90% Baltimore inmates, the other 10% were from surrounding counties.

In the federal system, you'll have inmates from everywhere in the United States of America.

In the State system, you got a choice to be in one of the local gangs.

In the Federal system, your involved in a gang one way or another, because the state in which your from is also considered a gang. That's why the last three digits on your ID # was important, so when you enter on the compound it gives verification of where you from.

In the State it's more like, if you're not running with a gang than you're pretty much on your own.

In the Fed's, if somebody out your state or gang that you run with is Fighting, than you better go and aid that person.

In the State system, you could be sent to any prison in that state.

In the Feds, the B.O.P. can send your ass out to space if they wanted to. If you wanted to be an asshole and keep getting into dumb shit in the prisons that you were sent to, the feds had a "get right program" for you. The program was called "Diesel Fuel", in which you are punished by being put on an airplane every 2-4 months and was sent to any prison in the U.S. By the time you got settled in one prison, you'd be back on the plane in another state before you knew it.

The feds are some cold hearted mother fuckas. First they kidnap you, send you far away from your family, and then only give you 300 minutes a month to call back home.

After about 2 weeks, I was finally called for Qaid. When I walked in the room, there were about 8 white staff members sitting at a long table waiting for me to join them. They all stared at me as if there was going to be a hanging.

The fat pale face one said, "are you Rome Walders?"

I said, "yeah".

The woman with the caked up makeup on her face said, "what are you incarcerated for?

I said, "Distribution of cocaine".

The Klans member across from me said,

"Do you want to go out into the population?"

I said, "yeah . . . . why would I want to stay in the S.H.U.?"

He said, "y'all seem to get into a lot of shit when y'all get on the compound".

The woman with the makeup caked on her face said, "what religion are you?"

"I don't have none", I replied.

The other members that shared the room, sat quietly and just stared at me the whole time.

Fat ass with the pale face said,

"send his ass to D-Block".

12 o'clock that evening, I was packed up, and on my way to the compound.

Lewisburg was nickname "The Big House", because every thing was inside the prison, the only reason you went outside was to the yard or to go to work.

There were 10 blocks in the prison, A-J. In front of every block there was a medal detector, as there was in any other part of the old penitentiary. There were cameras scattered everywhere through out Lewisburg, where as though you were under surveillance everywhere you went. "The eye", is what inmates called it, was always watching.

On each block there were 30 two man cells, on each of the three floors. There was a telephone room on the first floor.

Lewisburg population movement was controlled by a bell that went off every 10 minutes after the hour. On weekends and holidays, the bell went off every 20 minutes after the hour, after 4 o'clock everything went back to normal.

D-Block was the worst block in the old penitentiary. It was where the counselors sent all the "shot callers", and inmates who already had or were more likely to cause problems in the prison.

I use to hear the rap group "the lox" rap about D-block all the time, but they were just rapping. They couldn't visualize the things that I've witnessed and been through.

When I entered on D-Block, the tension was so thick, like invisible fog. Niggas stared and studied me like they were the jury and I was on trial.

The C.O. that ran the block was an asshole name "Murdoff", he signaled me to come into his office. The small room was the size of a small closet with a desk and a chair in it.

He said, "your going to be staying in cell#-318 . . . on the 3rd floor . . . in about an hour come back down here so I can send you to the laundry so you can get your bed roll, uniform etc . . ."

I started my journey to the 3rd floor, inmates was posted up everywhere.

"Where you come from my nigga?"

It seemed like I got asked that a million times.

"Baltimore", I repeatedly replied.

The first homie I ran into was from East Baltimore named "Butch". He was from Greenmount, and had been locked up with the feds for thirteen years.

After introducing ourselves to one another, he asked, "where you from yo?"

"Annapolis", I replied.

He said, "oh yeah . . . I know some bitches down there, where your cell at?"

"318", I replied.

He said, "you on the same floor as me, c'mon I'll take you up there".

While we walked to my cell, Butch introduced me to other homies on the block. When we got to where I would be staying, he said,

["you in the cell with "Yubi" . . . he the E-man for the Muslims . . . he's alright".]

I said, "as long as he ain't in my way, I'm a stay out his way".

[He said, "it's best that you get in a cell with a homie, because if the Muslims start beefing with one of the other gangs, niggas might run in here to stab your celly and fuck around hit you up in the mix of things".

I agreed. With a serious look on my face I said,

"I'm a need a knife".

He said, "I got one down in my cell for you, I give it to you later".

We sat in my cell while Butch broke down the do's and don'ts in the penitentiary, and the importance of your P.S.I paper work.

*[Your P.S.I. was everything. Before you get sentenced, the judge would send a probation officer to interview you, then they would report back to the judge. [More importantly, it'll show if you received any downward departures for cooperating with the feds.]

Before 02', if you entered in any Federal Penitentiary without your P.S.I, you were suspected of being a "Snitch". When the feds got word that lockups were so packed because inmates were getting "sent up top" (Checked in) because they couldn't show the proper paper work, B.O.P decided to take all P.S.I's out of the federal prisons altogether. Now, the feds got inmates worried to death trying to figure out who's Hot and who's not.

* [The Federal inmates out of the Baltimore car (group), got this thing that we called the "net" (internet). We used this technique since we couldn't verify if somebody was hot or not do the B.O.P making P.S.I's contraband in their prisons. Every federal system in the U.S. has someone from Baltimore who can call back to the city and get information on someone. If that's not enough, inmates who leave the supermax that come

into the system always got information on people regardless of what part of Maryland they were from. ⌐

The next best paper work an inmate can have is their "transcripts", everything that was said at your sentence was on these papers.

⌐ Snitching, fucking with faggots, stealing, running up a gambling debt, drugs or any other type of bills are all causes of your homies running you up top.⌐

There were so many gangs in Lewisburg Penitentiary, even religion was a gang. The Muslims was one of the deepest gangs in the federal prisons. Butch also informed me that Baltimore and D.C. were in alliance with each other. I was surprised at that because in the Maryland State system the two are always trying to kill each other. I guess in the feds that's a smart move because the two towns were only about 45 minutes away from each other. Plus, when its time to go to war, niggas going to need all the aiding they can get.

"bang, bang, bang!"

About an hour later, a knock came at the door.

Murdoff said, "Walders . . . I thought I told you to come back down in an hour so that you could go to the laundry?"

I said, "it ain't been an hour".

He said, "what you trying to say I can't tell time?"

Butch said, "c'mon Murdoff . . . he just got here, I was letting him know some important information about the penitentiary".

Murdoff said, "next time your ass going to the S.H.U.".

My blood pressure rose as the anger and rage showed on my face from letting this C.O. talk to me like that.

Butch saw the look on my face and knew that I was about to say something stupid, He hurried up and said,

"c'mon shorty . . . I'll take you down there".

When we walked off of the block, Butch saw that I was still in my feelings.

He said, "shorty . . . you can't let these C.O.'s get to you, because all they gonna do is make it harder for you while you're here. You got to remember that this is their house". Still in my feelings I said,

"I'm good".

The hallways in Lewisburg were crowded with inmates trying to get out to the yard so that they can claim their weights or to other activities that the old penitentiary had to offer.

During our journey, I was introduced to about 10 homies, all said that they would send me supplies. Butch told me don't look for it because they tell every new homie the same thing and don't send anything. I don't need anything from nobody, I was good, money was gonna stay in my account.

The laundry room was down stairs pass the barber shop, next to the inside gym.

Butch pointed out a dark spot in the hallway, which was one out of a million at Lewisburg, where inmates would commit illegal acts.

After getting my bed roll etc, we headed back to D-Block.

[Butch said, "whenever you ready to take a shower let me or one of the homies know, because the showers is one of the death traps on D-Block . . . so much shit be happening that you'll have to have a homie posted up outside of the shower door just incase niggas act up".]

I said, "Alright".

[He said, "oh yeah . . . keep your boots on going and coming from the shower"]

I agreed, because this wasn't my first time being locked up, I was always prepared for war.

When we got back to the third floor, Butch said, "I'm a let you put your stuff away . . . I'm going to go and get that sword (knife) for you.

I said, "alright".

When I got back to my cell, my cell buddy was sitting on his bed reading the "Koran". He greeted me by saying, "I'm Yubi brother".

I said, "I'm Booh".

Yubi was an older, little bit on the heavy side Muslim from Chicago, who had been incarcerated by the feds for about 15 years. The life sentence plus 30 years was handed down to him for murder and the attempt on some gangstaz that tried to rob him back in the windy city.

He said, "where you coming from brother?"

"Baltimore", I replied.

He said, "you met any of your homies yet?"

I said, "Butch been introducing me to homies since I stepped foot on the block".

He said, "yeah, Butch a good dude".

"Issue Allah", is what he spoke after everything he said. I wasn't a Muslims, but I agreed on some of the things that they taught. The one thing that I never understood was that the Koran teaches the Muslim Community to love their brother, family, and have unity. But, in the federal prisons they'll protect the same snitch that got someone taken away from their family.

After making my bed and putting my property away, Butch took me upstairs to show me the T.V. room.

There were 5 T.V's in the large room, but all were separated off from each other so that it would be less altercations. There was a B.E.T, movie, news, sports, and a telemundo T.V. for the Spanish inmates. Majority of the black inmates spent Mon-fri from 6 p.m.-8p.m. at Lewisburg in the B.E.T. room watching "Rocsi" on 106 and park, hoping to see a back shot of her little bony ass. Even though you had to use your Walkman to enjoy the sound, the noises that the inmates created would always remind you that you were in a penitentiary. Even though there was the eye in the sky always watching your every move, the T.V. room was also used as a battle field. Butch informed me that table games and sports were two of the main reasons. There were blood stains on the floor and walls in the room.

The rats and mice that used this T.V. room as their home, scented the area with the smell of their piss and shit.

The birds would pay a visit from the hole in the roofs which showed that the old castle was long over due to be torn down. Whenever it would rain, you'd have to use the mop buckets to catch the water so that the room wouldn't get flooded.

★ The chow (lunch room) was big as shit at Lewisburg. The shot callers at the prison way before I got there, came to agreements on where each gang would sit while eating in the area, so that there would be no altercations. The Baltimore car sat in the green section, which was a death trap because it was in the middle of the area.

Another homie I became cool with was from Murphy homes named, "Fox". He was a soulja. We connected with each other without a problem at all. All Fox did was make fun of people all day, funny mother fucka. Soon as a nigga would invite him to fight, Fox would gladly accept their invitation and show them how nice he was with his hands. If the feds wouldn't have locked him up for being an enforcer for the crew he ran with, he would've easily been on T.V. showing his boxing skills to the world. The 39 year old, same height as me, Muslim said that I reminded him of his co-defendant in his case that got found guilty of the "Rico Law". Fox got 25 years back in 2001, he wasn't going to lay down though. He was fighting to get back in court and give the time back. The Muslims kicked him out of their community several times for him making the statement that "snitches join the Muslim community so that they could be protected in the prisons." He didn't care though, he'd rather pray to "Allah" by himself. He always said,

"just because you go to the mosque (place of prayer) don't make you a Muslim."

When the 2 o'clock bell rang, I went to the counselors office which seemed like a mile from D-block.

My appointed counselor's name was "Mr. Murphy." The medium size, bald head, white man who smelled like cigars, explained to me the reason why I had penitentiary points.

He said, "a new point system went into effect early this year. The younger you are, the more points B.O.P. gives you, add them points to your criminal history points along with your time and that's how you got 26 points. Twenty four points and over sends you to the penitentiary. If you stay out of trouble in the next two years . . . I'll more then likely lower your points and send you to a medium security prison."

The look on my face showed of disappointment from hoping that B.O.P had made a mistake with my points. "Fuck it though, it is what it is. I could adapt to any environment or situation.

The way that inmates were living at Lewisburg Penitentiary wasn't normal. The cell doors opened up at 5:10am every morning just like clock work, unless the institution was on lockdown. To be safe you had to put your chair in front of your doorway just in case a rival gang tried to sneak attack while you were sleeping. The chair would at least give you a couple of seconds to prepare for war. After a couple of weeks of witnessing what seemed like non stop stabbings, fights and assaults, my counselor wasted no time getting me a job in the kitchen.

Monday-Friday from 4am-12:30pm, for only $5 a month I was in the dirty chow area watching inmates trying to steal any and everything that wasn't bolted down. The Mexicans didn't care what they stole, instead of going back to the block empty handed, they'd take napkins or salt and pepper shakers. Inmates would steal sugar, raw meat, etc., then would hide it in different spots until they could make it back to the block. 9 times out of 10, the mice or the rats would get to their stash and have a feast with it. Inmates didn't care though, they'd still take it back to the blocks and sell it or eat it themselves.

Ms. Rollow, who we called "swollow", because she had some dick sucking lips, was in charge of the kitchen on the shift I was working. She was about 5 feet tall, white woman in her late 20's, a beat up body, with a face only a mother could love. The inmates at Lewisburg didn't care though, to them she was an angel who had fell from heaven. Swallow always used to say,

"I couldn't see myself with a blackman."

Let her tell it, but she had no problem with rubbing up against a nigga dick or talking nasty to him. Swallow was alright though, as long as you did your work, and nobody got stabbed or assaulted on her shift, she really didn't give a fuck what you were doing in the kitchen. She would sit there and let the perverted inmates "gun her down" (Masturbate). On days when she wasn't in the mood, she'd get that individual sent to lock up.

If you were working on the serving line, it was possible that you were going to get into an altercation with an inmate for talking slick because you wouldn't add more food on their plate. We called it "the line of death," because when serving on that line you had to deal with about 1,000 different attitudes. Inmates had been getting killed for something as little as serving food at the old penitentiary since back in the late 30's.

My job was cleaning up the middle section of the kitchen. I didn't mind because I didn't have to deal with niggas, and plus I practically slept most of the time.

Outside of the kitchen was known as the "red top" and the white boys used it as a call for help to the C.O.'s. White gangs knew that they were the minority in the penitentiary, so whenever they wanted to punish a nigger, they'd do it in front of the C.O's main bubble which was on the red top. That way by the time any African Americans realized what was going on, the riot squad would already be there to terminate the situation.

Any given time in the penitentiary you might have to take a persons life because they just wanted to test you or you just wanted to test them. I knew a lot of inmates who came into Lewisburg with a light sentence, but ran their time up by killing, stabbing, and sexually assaulting other inmates or staff.

In Lewisburg, you had a choice to be a predator or prey. 98% of the inmates in the penitentiary were predators that preyed on the weak 2%. Lewisburg was so bad that the predators preyed on other predators because there weren't enough weak inmates to go around. The old castle was a "death trap." If the B.O.P. sent you to Lewisburg Federal Penitentiary, you were sent there to get killed.

There were two separate racial riots that occurred during my stay. The Muslims went to war with the Mexicans, and the D.C. inmates forced the dirty white boys to check in after a small riot.

I remembered my mother broke down and cried the first time she came to see me in the penitentiary. The wall that surrounded the prison or the Carolina blue jump suit I had on would've made any mother look at their child as being on death row. Whenever she and other loved ones would visit they all said that when they entered the prison they felt the evil in the air. It was rumored that the prison was built on top of a grave yard.

I moved in the cell with Butch after his cell buddy went home. Butch was catching (smuggling) a lot of dope in Lewisburg from the loved ones that visited him. A lot of homies hated the fact that he was getting money even though he always shared with them, they always wanted more. The jealousy and envy brought a lot of hate to the penitentiary, but it was no where near to what the heroine was bringing. Just imagine having some dope in your pocket in a caged area, with nothing but fiends watching your every move. That shit would be real stressful, and as soon as you sleep the boldest fiends got their arms stretched out with their hands reaching for your throat. That's exactly how it was everyday at Lewisburg Penitentiary, if you got some heroine in your possession. About six months later, our cell got "shook down" (searched) because a dope fiend was caught with a "dirty" (failed drug test) and decided to snitch on Butch.

Murdoff said, "step out of the cell"

Butch said, "why you fucking with us early this morning?"

Murdoff said, "somebody dropped a note (snitched) and said y'all got some dope in the cell"

We looked at each other and both said, "What!"

After about a half hour search, Murdoff found the sword that was under Butch's pillow.

With the sharp object in his hand he said,

"what's this?"

With a smart voice Butch said, "what it look like?"

Murdoff let out a little laugh then said,

"y'all go head to the lieutenants office."

While sitting on the lieutenants bench, Butch informed me that he was going to take the charge so I didn't have to worry about nothing. It was a good thing I let a homie use my knife the day before, because if I hadn't it would've been two instead of one he would've found.

When we got into the office, lieutenant Johnson was sitting in his chair with his feet up on top of the desk. With the Grand Wizard look on his face he said,

"which one of y'all going to take this knife charge?"

Butch spoke up and said, "that knife is mine."

Johnson stood and said, "well here's the thing. Both of y'all going to the S.H.U. until my staff finish searching the cell because I got some information that y'all got some drugs in there."

Butch said, "why you going to lock both us up if I told you I'm a take the knife charge, because ain't no drugs in the cell."

Johnson said, "y'all heard me . . . Murdoff take their asses to the S.H.U."

After being strip searched and handed orange jumpers, we were taken to our cell on lock up.

The hot August heat had us feeling like crabs in a hot pot. Every move that you made in the cell, the sweat would run down your body like somebody was spraying you with a small water hose. The old penitentiary had no air condition, the little breeze that we got from our cell window teased us 24 hours everyday.

The warden and the counselors came to the S.H.U to make their rounds every Wednesday to see if any inmates had any requests or concerns. Our block counselor handed both of us a piece of paper to inform us that we were under investigation for drugs.

Butch said, "yo . . . ain't nobody drop a note on us but a homie."

I said, "Damn! . . . . Niggas be getting down like that?"

He said, "homies always been jealous of me because they know I be making moves (smuggling drugs) . . . lil Booh besides going to war with rival gangs. The only real problems that you'll have in the penitentiary is with your own homies. When your labeled as being a homie you open the door for niggas that's in your circle. They might start playing with you or certain shit that they would say to you they wouldn't say or do it to a rival gangs because they know that it would more than likely start a war, that homie shit is over rated." It was always said that Baltimore, Detroit and New Orleans Niggas act the same because they're all heroin cities, 90% of the inmates in the federal system carried that same dope fiend mentality.

I asked Butch, "how long they can keep us down here for being under investigation?

He said, "we gotta wait to see the D.H.O (Discipline housing officer) who would decide the punishment for the shot (charge). I'm a still take the knife charge. The only reason you in here with me is because the lieutenant think its some dope in the cell."

The days dragged on and on. The hot summer heat had me feeling like a bee trapped in a jar with just one pin hole at the top of it. The small 10 x 4 cell lacked oxygen, it had me spending most of my days with my head pressed against the window trying to get as much air as possible.

After 30 days of what seemed like living in hell from the heat, hearing inmates, moans, screaming, and cries, we were called to see the D.H.O, after a short while in the room, Butch came out and said,

"you good Shorty . . . I took care of that."

The C.O. behind him told me to pack my shit because I was going back on the compound.

Butch informed me that the D.H.O. took 45 good days from him and gave him 45 more days in the S.H.U.

At 1 o'clock that September evening, I was back on D-Block.

I was put in the cell with "G-Man." He was originally from Kingston Jamaica, but moved to Jamaica Queens in Yankeeville with his family when he was 7 years old. Americanized is what he said he was because he had been in America so long he could speak better English then the Jamaican language. He was a "rude boy" (gangsta), good dude though. Besides the snoring, we got along well. All G-man wanted to do was talk about Jamaica and say "Blood clot" all day. Since I've vacationed on the island we would reminisce with each other about it almost every night. Being that it was a good chance that the 45 year old, 6 foot tall, with dreads that came down his back, wouldn't step foot in Jamaica again because of the 3 life sentences that was handed down to him 10 years ago for murders in Yankeeville. I somewhat eased his mind because all he and most of the inmates at Lewisburg could do was imagine life as a convict, that's getting old. Where I'm from, we call it being buried alive or doing the wheel.

Besides the corrupted, criminal minded, evil souls that called the old penitentiary their home, there were also some important individuals at Lewisburg. Every hustler knows that in the feds there are a million and one connects that you could get plugged into. So in reality, if the judge gave you a sentence that you could see day light, the B.O.P is practically introducing you to a connect that could send you product once you got back into society.]

The big Miami Cocaine drug dealer "Willie Falcon" slept across from me on D-block, good dude. He loved Maryland, he always said that we were souljas, and had swagger like no other.]

Kenneth "Supreme" McGridd was on G-Block (Gang Unit) in which he had to stay there for 18 months to complete the program because he was labeled as being high profile. Everybody who was in the cell with him that came out on the compound said that all he talked about was how Curtis "50 cent" Jackson is a coward. In a magazine article, 50 cent was suppose to have said that Supreme was at Lewisburg penitentiary and scared to go out to the yard. 50 cent must not have known that it was impossible for Supreme to come out to the yard or compound because of his sentence status.] ✳ ✳ ✳ ✳

It seemed like every Yankee inmate at Lewisburg tried to get the lieutenant to let him out on the compound after he finished the program. Lieutenant Johnson stayed with his word and said that it wasn't going to happen though. It was rumored that the Ja-Rule featuring lil Wayne video was the main reason, because at the end of the video everybody had Supreme Team on their shirts. Inmates say that Johnson saw that as being a security risk. The leader of the Notorious "Supreme Team" gang from Queens, NY was serving a life sentence which was handed to him a couple of years back. "TUT" was another individual at Lewisburg that had issues with 50 cent, because the rapper mentioned his name on the song "Many Men." Real niggas called it dry snitching.] ✳ ✳ ✳

✳✳ One individual who was in the same car I was in was "Rudy Williams." Rudy was one of the biggest heroin dealers that came out of Baltimore City, good dude. Every chance I got, I talked to Rudy about legitimate business because he was definitely a person who I could get some priceless knowledge from. The old man was a soulja, and it wasn't hard to tell because his reputation followed him in the penitentiary. It seemed like everybody gave him much respect.

✳ I got somewhat star struck when I got introduced to the hungarian drug lord name "Malvo." He was a billionaire, a connects connect, and reminded me so much of the connect I had back home (Blonco). Malvo couldn't even speak English, all he did was smile and motion his head up and down. He got extradited too the U.S. 4 years ago on drug conspiracy charges from which a judge gave him six life sentences. The government was that crazy knowing that Malvo was well in his 80's, and a 10 year sentence would easily send him to his maker.

My brother and Muse came to see me at the old castle to keep me informed about how the family was doing, while I was away. Black said, "Damn yo . . . you getting big as shit!"

"Thanks my nigga", I replied

Muse said, "yo . . . you cut up like a big bag of dope."

We all let out the hyena laugh, it was always good to see some familiar faces from back home. Both assured me that the family was maintaining, doing well, and couldn't wait for my arrival. Black informed me that he had run into a Cuban who was staying up Baltimore that had some good cocaine and that the price was kind of high but it was worth it.

[Muse informed me that the family had a small problem with some niggas calling themselves the "realaz" but the hyenas quickly took care of it.]

I asked, "how the little one doing?"

Black said, "that nigga doing good. He told me to tell you he love you and can't wait until you come home."

Muse said, "every party we go to, the little one manage too get the microphone and send a shout out to you."

Black said, "that little nigga always wearing a shirt with your picture on the front, and free lil booh on the back."

✱ [I said, "I want both y'all to promise me that y'all gonna make sure he safe out there." Muse said, "that nigga safe yo . . . niggas ain't crazy."

Black said, "ain't nothing going to happen to that nigga before it happen to me first."

I said, "that's what's up."

✱ [Black said, "Oh yeah . . . I got word that Fabo and that nigga Low home"]

✱ [I said. "all them rat niggas should be home before me."

✱ Muse said, "how you want me to handle the situation?"

✱ I said, "Nawh . . . don't fuck wit none of them . . . I'm a take care of them personally."]

For about five hours we reminisced about back in the days. Finally I informed them that the drug game was over for me, and that I had plans on getting legal money when I get home. They tried to hide the disappointed look on their faces, but they knew by little-h being family and one of the main reasons why I was in federal prison, damaged me mentally. I was scared because when I was out there hustling, I was married to the game, that bitch was the one who broke her vows, for that reason alone, the streets owed me and I wanted my payment in blood.

The visiting time went so fast, when it was time to go I could see the sadness in their eyes. After giving them both a brotherly hug, I assured them that I would be home in no time. Every inmate at Lewisburg penitentiary was involved in "criminal activity" one way or another. There was no such thing as halfway crooks. I stayed at the old penitentiary for 2 years, and by the grace of God, I made it through without a scratch on me.

Every single day at the penitentiary was a life or death situation for inmates who used Lewisburg as their home. I witnessed weak inmates walk light because they didn't want to piss the ground off, or they acted like they were walking on a tight rope. Could you imagine being dropped off in the middle of the jungle with wild animals all around you every day trying to prey on you, and all you have is a knife to protect yourself with. That's how inmates lived everyday at Lewisburg. The old castle was a concrete jungle and if you showed any weakness, niggas was coming for you. Adapt or die. Being in a place like that all day made your heart frozen one way or another.

That was an experience in my life that I'll never forget.

CHAPTER 44

Fairton, Jersey

On that mild September day at 8 o'clock in the morning, I was on a bus getting transferred to a medium security prison.

When I left out of the old penitentiary, it felt like a 1,000 pounds had been lifted off of my shoulders.

While we traveled, my eyes stared out the window into society like a new born baby, who was seeing the world for the first time.

The 2 years that I stayed at Lewisburg, whenever I went outside to the yard to work out or walk the track, all I could see was the big wall that surrounded the penitentiary.

About 4 hours later, we were at the air lift in Harrisburg. I didn't have a clue where I was going, all I could do was hope that it was somewhere close to Maryland.

After going through the same procedures as my last air lift visit, my name was called and I was guided to another bus. I found a seat in the back next to a Muslim named, "Mustafah". He was from Philly and had just done 16 years at "Bomount Penitentiary", which was another killing field. By looking at his gray beard and seeing in the dark spots underneath his eyes, it wasn't hard to tell that the penitentiary had gotten the best of him.

After greeting each other he asked,

"where you coming from?"

"Lewisburg", I replied

After telling me where he came from, how long he had been gone and what he was charged with, he informed me that the bus we were on was going to New Jersey, either "Fortdix or Fairton." I was alright with that because both of the prisons were close to Maryland.

He said, "for me to be going to a medium security facility is a blessing . . . Issue Allah."

✗[Mustafah knew that it was a good chance that he'd die in a federal prison due to the life sentence plus 5 years that was handed down to him for his roll in a drug deal gone bad in which an undercover officer was murdered.]

After about a 3 hour nap, I woke up at FDC (federal detention center) in Philly. While the exchange of inmates were being made, every inmate on the bus witnessed the sexy black and Korean females that walked pass the bus. Most of them shook their ass a little harder once they noticed they had an audience of inmates watching their every move.

After leaving the F.D.C. we went to Fairton, New Jersey in about 3 hours. My first reaction when I saw the prison was that it looked like a college campus, and the trees they had on the compound made it almost official. Instead of having a big ass wall surrounding the prison like the Penitentiary, there were two razor sharp fences that kept the inmates from escaping and intruders from entering.

Fairton was like a 5 star hotel compared to Lewisburg. The advantages of the prison were that it was more cleaner, they allowed movies every weekend, and the computers on the block allowed you to email your loved ones etc . . . Being down Fairton was like a breath of fresh air to anyone that came from a penitentiary.

There was only one area of medal detectors that you had to go through and less cameras watching your every move because there was less violence in the facility.

Being at this less security prison and the way it was being ran assured me that I'd be making it home from federal prison.

[The disadvantages that the facility had was that it was Rat (snitches) infested[And to top that, the B.O.P had a prison right behind Fairton that housed nothing but snitches. We called it the "cheese cake factory."]

The C.O's were prettier than at Lewisburg, and every week on inspection day if you got below average the T.V's would be turned off until a reasonable time.

Majority of the inmates that used Fairtion as their home, treated the facility like joining the army, "be all you can be." The prisonology talk was at an all time high. Everybody claimed they were getting money in their town. They had this, they got that. I was always the type of person that believed half of what I saw and none of what I heard.

Instead of having only two man cells, Fairton also had three, four, six, and even eight man cells. The facility was so laid back that the counselors would put you in a cell with anybody regardless of what gang or color you were. In any federal penitentiary, that wasn't going to happen due to the fact that racial wars could kick off at any given time.

Fairton medium security prison compound was controlled by an announcement that let you know when the move was on.

After being processed in and going through the normal procedures I was put on lock up because by me coming from a penitentiary, I had to wait until the captain approved me to go out on the compound.

My cell buddy was from south Philly named, "Rhinny." This was his second time coming back to Fairton for violating his probation. All he was sentenced to was six months, but the way he acted you would've thought that he had a fresh life sentence. All he did was literally cry all night about his wife who he said he had left out there on the streets. I practically had to tell him to "shut the fuck up" because he was starting to get me thinking about Monique and Sherica, and what my life would've been like if Tina hadn't got killed.

Monique and Sherica still showed me love through out my incarceration even though they were in other relationships. I was thankful for them both continuing to show me support because most hood stars who get locked up for playing the game, their females go when the money leave. Once the judge sentenced you and banged that gavel, that's when the females come back to reality and remember all the dirt you've done to them, and the lonely nights not knowing where you were or who you were with. So to them, the best way to get a nigga back was when he's down, off his feet. "Hell has no fury like a woman whose been scorned." They'll forgive you, but they don't forget.

As for those project bitches, they were like city buses, miss one next 15 minutes one coming. I guess in reality 99% of hustlers in this country are just being loved for breaking the law.

The next morning the C.O. came to my cell and told me to pack up because I was going out to the compound.

I was assigned to stay on A block. On the block there were about 150 inmates, six T.V's, 4 phones, a laundry room, 3 microwaves, and 4 computers.

I was assigned to a 3 man cell on the top floor. My two cell buddies were ok, "Murda" was from New Jersey, and "Jack was from Boston, we all were around the same age.

[After putting my supplies away, my cell buddies introduced me to a couple of my Baltimore homies that were on the block. The only 2 homies that got my attention were "Name-a" who was getting a lot of money in the city at a very young age, and who was also Rudy Williams nephew.]

[The other was one of Baltimore's biggest heroin dealers, Maurice "Peanut King." Even though he had been locked up before I was born, his name still rang in "B-More Murdaland" as if he had never left the streets.]

[Peanut King was in his early 50's but the energy that he had in his body would've told you different.[The 30 laps that he ran around the yards track almost every morning was a fact that his heart was as strong as a 21 year old. He had been locked up for 27 years, and by looking at him you could tell that he didn't let the incarceration time get to him. After we introduced ourselves to one another, Peanut said,

"Where you from Booh?"

"Annapolis," I replied

He said, "Naptown huh . . . you know Blew? He from near that area?"

I said, "Yeah . . . we were out Talbot county together."

Peanut informed me that Blew was on C-block, and I can go and holler at him when the move come on if I wanted too.]

Ten minutes later the move was called and I was on my way to C-block. Halfway to the block, I felt somebody grab my jacket. I didn't know anybody down here so my first reaction was to prepare myself to punish a nigga, when I turned around, I saw Blew smiling while saying,

"what's up yo?"

It took me a couple of seconds to come out of my penitentiary state of mind.

I said, "yo . . . don't do that . . . I didn't know who the fuck you was."

After greeting each other with a hand shake, we walked out to the yard.

I asked, "how you know I was down here?"

He said, "word travel fast . . . one of the homies told me you just came from Lewisburg and you was put on A-block."

Blew was well liked and known by all different people at Fairton, and for that reason alone a lot of homies didn't like him. It was the same way at Lewisburg, if you known for making moves and getting money, niggas out your circle always going to hate on you.

[The yard was about the same size as Lewisburgs, but instead of one, Fairton had two baseball fields.]

The weight pile was smaller than at Lewisburg, but the good thing about it was that the weights weren't chained up like at the federal penitentiaries.

That day, Blew and I walked the track for about 3 hours reminiscing about back in the days. We talked about everything that had happened in our lives, and what our plans were when we got back into society. [This was Blews first time being incarcerated, so everything he was going through I had already been through. All the advice I was giving him about his situations was all certified.

I could always joke to Blew about the time when I was going to get him slumped. [He was a good sport about the situation because that was in the past and now we were cool with each other.] The homies called us "county boys," but not being disrespectful because they knew that we were souljas, and had each others back.

It took me a while to adjust to Fairton because unlike the penitentiary, you had to think for these inmates most of the time. I witnessed the stupid shit that they would do all day that would've got them chopped up at Lewisburg.

[The rat infested niggas would go back and fourth to court and wouldn't even bring any paper work back to state the reason why they left. In my mind, 99% of the inmates on the compound couldn't be trusted, I stayed out their way and they definitely stayed out mine.

[The 25 years that was handed down to Blew 3 years ago didn't seem to bother him much. He was sure that when his appeal went through that he would be going home in a couple of years. The technique that he used at his trial did no justice for his case. Him and all the other inmates that tried that "U.C.C." was fed false hope. They had to be out of their mind to think that the government was just going to open the prison doors and release inmates because the constitution clearly explains that the way the feds were incarcerating individuals was wrong.

[It seemed like the inmates at Fairton were going home everyday, while in the penitentiary it was rare that you heard of an inmate going back to society.]

So that I could stay focused at Fairton, I took an outside college course at Ashworth University, where I received my associates degree in Business. From a young age I developed the brain of a businessman, but I felt that if I had a degree it would make me more official out in society. "a fool and his money will always part ways."

The late great "Rev. Martin Luther King Jr." once said, "Intelligence and character is a good goal to getting a good education."

[After 2 years of me being at the medium security prison, Black and Muse came to visit me. When they came to see me at Lewisburg they brought good news, by the look on their faces this time I could tell that something was wrong.

I said, "five months and 23 days left for me to go to the halfway house to be exact . . . I can't wait to get up out here."

I leaned back in my chair and looked back and forth at both of them and said,

"tell me what's wrong"

Black took a deep breath and then said,

["The family is in bad shape."

I said, "Bad shape how?"

Black said, "the Cuban connect I was buying weight from, got killed up Baltimore last month and now we trying to find another connect."

I have been watching lately on the news how the Mexican cartels have been going to war with each other over the drug route to America. [Lately the D.E.A. been closing down the routes that the cartels used for bringing their drugs over to the so called, "land of opportunity." That's the main reason why Mexico had close to 8,000 murders last year alone. The thirst for the American dollar had the cartels killing each other over the remaining routes, and that's one of the main reasons why it was so hard to find a connect and why prices of cocaine were so high.]

I said, "the family been hustling all this time, so take a break until I get home and I'll see to it that y'all be straight. Don't get it twisted because I'm not getting back into the drug game. I'm going to just turn y'all on to the connect I had when I was home."

Black said, "it ain't that easy my nigga"

I said, "why ain't it. I know y'all niggas been saving y'all money up . . . right?"

Muse cut in and said, "we been saving our money Shorty. Its just if we take a break until you come home five months from now, the family might not have any more clientele to sell weight too."

I stared at Muse and said,

"what you mean?"

Black said, "the last time we came too see you in the penitentiary I told you that it was some niggas that came down Naptown calling themselves the 'Realaz' trying to move in on the projects"

With a killer look on my face I looked at Muse and said, "I thought y'all said that them niggas wasn't a problem?"

Muse said, "they wasn't a problem, but if the family don't have product to sell to niggas how is it that we are going to keep niggas from buying from them?"

I said, "where these niggas from?"

Black said, "a bitch from out Annapolis Gardens that I fuck every once in a while say that them niggas part of the New Orleans crime wave . . . the main nigga is supposedly named "reala-rodney" or "Rodney Reala.""

Muse said, "all them niggas from out the Realaz family put the Reala on the end of their names so that niggas know who they is."

Black said, "I got a good look at the nigga Rodney last week at the stop light . . . he was driving a silver Bentley. When I was about to jump out the car and slump him, a police car pulled up at the intersection."

Muse said, "I heard he just slumped a nigga from out parole a couple of weeks ago for addressing him as Rodney Reals?"

I said, "I thought the nigga name was Rodney-Reala?"

Muse said, "people say that Rodney Reala is what his comrades called him . . . but if you ain't a reala, he wanted you to address him as Reala-Rodney because everything he do is supposed to be real. And it's supposed to represent how him and his souljas survived Hurricane Katrina after the government left them to die."

Black said, "these niggas some clowns . . . they on some geographic shit."

The anger that I had inside of me showed by the expression on my face. I looked at Muse then said,

"Send them hyenas to find out where that nigga Rodney at and make him wish he never stepped foot in Naptown."

Muse said, "I'm on it."

I said, "once you chop off the head of the snake, the whole body fall."

I told Black in the mean time in between time, try and find a connect that can just hold the family above water until I get to this halfway house. He agreed.

I told Muse that after the hyenas slumped that nigga Rodney, if any other Realaz looking for revenge then show them how real the family is.

After giving both of them a brotherly hug, I walked out of the visiting room still disturbed about how niggas try to come and muscle their way into the Capital of Maryland.

The months dragged on and on. Blew's appeal had finally came through and he was due back in court in November.

About a month after my visit, Black informed me that the hyenas found that nigga Rodney down Robinwood and put about 20 bullet holes in his body. Witnesses say that he had so much lead in him that he looked like a human pencil when the ambulance pulled him out of the car. He also informed me that the other so called "Realaz" dissappeared after they heard their boss got slumped.

Black had found a connect up Yankeeville just to supply enough cocaine to last the family until I cam home. The product he was getting wasn't all that good, but it was average enough for niggas to sell.

★   ★   ★

God sat on the couch in his condo eating shrimp dipped in tomato soup, he couldn't get gumbo in Maryland no where so he had to settle for less.

"ring . . . ring . . . ring"

He picked up the phone and said,

"hello"

His lieutenant on the other line named Pone said,

"God-Reala . . . I got some bad news."

God hated to be put on hold when somebody was giving him bad news. With an impatient voice he said,

"spit it out Woe-dey!"

With a fragile voice Pone said,

"your brother just got killed."

God jumped up off of the couch not caring about the shrimp falling on his $10,000 white carpet that he loved so much, and said,

"killed where?"

Pone said, "I got a call saying that he got shot about 20 times down Naptown while he was sitting in his car by some niggas known as the Family."

God yelled, "come pick me up out White Marsh Now!"

After throwing the phone violently against the wall, God dropped his helpless body on the couch, still in shock that his little brother was just killed. To add insult to injury, he thought how he was going to tell his mother that her youngest son was going to come back to her in a box.

The ride to Naptown was quiet. Pone and the other Realaz could've easily revenged Rodney's death because to them revenge was like the sweetest joy next to getting pussy, but God wanted to take care of this situation personally. He felt as though it would've some what eased the pain he was feeling from loosing his brother to a lifestyle in which he got him involved. All God could think about was Rodney's helpless body being slumped in the Bentley that he had bought him for his birthday. After being hit by so many bullets, niggas was going to pay. Any and everybody who had anything to do with the so called "family" was going to be pushing up flowers. The only thing that's worse then crossing a line is not knowing you've crossed it.

Ring . . . Ring . . . Ring

Pone answered his cell phone and said,

"Yeah"

On the other end of the phone a females voice said,

"Pone this Tisha."

Pone cut her off by saying, "bitch . . . you address me like you supposed too."

With a fragile voice she said, "Reala-Pone, I'm sorry for leaving the Reala out."

With anger in his voice Pone said,

"Bitch don't let it happen again . . . now what the fuck you got for me?"

Tisha said, "the only nigga from out the family that's out here is little one."

Pone looked at his boss and said,

"God-Reala . . . this a bitch I be fucking down Naptown and she say the only nigga that's out there from the Family is a nigga named Little One."

Without even looking at his lieutenant, God said,

"he'll due."

Pone got back on the phone and said,

"don't let that nigga go no where . . . we be down there in about an hour."

God had never killed anybody before, beating niggas down with bats or kicking the shit out of a person wasn't the same as killing someone. For him, he knew that murder was going to be a tough thing to digest, but once he knew that his brother got killed he would have to commit the act, all the murders that were committed during their stay in Maryland were done by the Realaz, all God had to do was point and the Realaz would've squeezed the trigger without even thinking twice.

Following four car loads behind their boss, the Realaz were angry and anxious to avenge their kin folks death. They didn't give a fuck who was out there, kids, old people, they didn't care. God pointed. The choppers they carried were going to chop that person up. They were going to make sure that Naptown would remember the Realaz.

After selling his last piece of crack rock, Little one decided to call it a night. It was getting late outside, plus after 12 o'clock it wasn't nothing but trouble over Eastport. During the grave yard shift it was the stick-up niggas time to claim the projects. From across the street he noticed Tisha's phat ass. Little one had been wanting too fuck her for a while now, but she would always tell him that he was too young. Little One didn't have a problem with buying the pussy, especially tonight after just making close to $5,000.

Little-One hollered. "Tisha . . . Tisha . . . let me holler at you."

He then went and sat in his car over Harbor House in the pool parking lot and watched her phat red ass walk towards him.

He said, "when you going let me fuck you?"

Tisha said, "boy . . . I told you that you were too young for me to be fucking wit."

Tisha was a female out A.G. (Annapolis Gardens) who in the past decided to make her career out of the oldest profession known to man kind, prostitution. She was a sexy red bone and looked like the singer Alicia Keys, but with some bigger breasts. Her long pretty hair came down to her ass, and yeah it was real.

Out of towners would fall in love with the Nubian Goddess because only the hustlers in Naptown knew how shiesty she was. Tisha would get paid by the stars in Naptown to set up niggas who try to come down and claim goldmine in the city. Most of the time niggas would get robbed, but it was also rumored that she was the reason why five Yankees were murdered a couple of years back. While the lame niggas would be getting a good fuck from Tisha, she would be plotting on them the whole time.

✳ [Everything Tisha knew about the streets, she had learned from her mother, who was the Annapolis High School class of '78 Prom Queen,] but now she was nothing but a crack fiend. Her father had been doing a life sentence at the "Cut Annex" ever since she was 3 years old for murder in the 1st degree.]

Tisha was a female hustler, who was using her body to get what she wanted. She wore all the stylish clothing, and had a mean shoe game. She was still a lost black girl because her last month abortion was one out of five in the past. Instead of using the money that she was making to get out of the projects, so that she could be something in life, she was satisfied with living in the housing authority and running the streets.

Little-One had heard stories about how good Tish'a pussy was from a lot of hustlers and he wanted to see if the rumors were true.

He said, "That's crazy how you treating me Tisha."

She said, "when you get a couple of years older . . . holler at me."

Knowing that Little One wasn't going to make in through the night, because she knew Pone and the Realaz wasn't going to take it kindly that one of their brothers was killed.

With anger in his voice from knowing that Tisha wasn't going to give him the pussy.

He said, "fuck it then . . . I'm gone." then he started up his car.

She knew that Pone was going to be mad at her if she allowed Little one to leave before he got down there. The last thing she wanted to do was get on his bad side, because to her Pone was her meal ticket.

Tisha said, "hold up!"

Little One said, "hold up for what?"

[She said, "I'll tell you what . . . give me $100 and I'll let you grab on my ass for a couple minutes."]

That got Little One's attention. After cutting the car off and giving out a hyena laugh he said, "alright."

Tisha said, "give me my money first."

Little One reached in his pocked, pulled out $100 bill then handed it to her.

She took the money, then turned around and said,

"hurry up"

After giving out another hyena laugh, Little One leaned out of the car window and reached his arms so his hand could get a good grip on Tisha's soft round perfect ass. The spandex pants that she had on hugged her ass so tight that any blind man would've thought that she was ass naked. Little One's dick got harder as he continued to message her ass. He didn't let the moment get interrupted, when Tisha's cell phone rang. While continuing to let Little One feel all up in her ass she answered the phone.

"Hello"

Pone said, "we up here where you at?"

She said, "I'm in the pool parking lot."

Not paying attention to Tisha on the phone, Little One continued to rub the crack of her ass like it was no tomorrow, he thought to himself, "fuck this . . . I'm ready to jerk off . . . I can't let this moment pass."

After Tisha got off the phone, she turned around and said, "alright, times up."

With one hand in his pants and the other out the window Little One said, "hold up . . . let me touch it for one more minute?"

Tisha leaned towards the inside of the car to see what he was doing. After smiling, she said,

"oh you jerking off . . . that's another $100.00."

With a disappointed look on his face Little One said,

"Bitch . . . you crazy if you think I'm going to give you more money without even touching the pussy."

Right after that was said, Little One noticed four cars head lights driving up towards them.

He said, "who the fuck is that?"

She said, "I don't know."

Before he knew it, the cars had him trapped and he couldn't drive off even if he wanted too. When he turned to look at Tisha she was no where in sight.

Pone jumped out of the car pointed the chopper at Little One then said, "don't move Woe-dey"

The Realaz followed suit and surrounded Little One's car like bees surrounded honey.

With the heart of a lion, Little One mugged his face at Pone then said, "fuck you want nigga?"

Pone just stared at Little One while grinding his teeth.

Little One said, "what y'all want some money nigga?"

It took all of Pone's strength not to pull the trigger and watch this little nigga head explode like a watermelon, he knew this situation was personal and God wanted to handle the problem himself.

After convincing himself what he had to do, God got out of the car and walked next to Pone. He looked at Little One and then grabbed the chopper from his lieutenant. After pointing the assault rifle at Little One he said, "this is for my brother."

Little One said, "Nigga I don't know you or your brother . . . BANG, BANG, BANG, BANG!"

[Before he could finish his sentence the chopper went off and brain pieces scattered inside the car.]

Pone looked at Little One's dead body then said,

"now that a get'cha mind right."

God gave Pone back the chopper then said,

"let's get the fuck outta here."

C h a p t e r   4 5

Adding Insult To Injury

I met Blew out in the yard to walk the track for the last time, around this time tomorrow I'll be in the halfway house in B-more.

Blew said, "what's up my nigga?

"I got my glasses on waiting for the sun to shine," I replied

He said, "hell yeah . . . You been waiting for tomorrow to come for a while now."

I said, "you be home in a couple of months after you go back to court."

He said, "hopefully they chop this 25 years down so we can be uptown together and shit on them snitch ass niggas."

I said, "fuck them Sammy the Bull ass niggas . . . once they hear I'm on my way home, they already know what it's hitting for."

During the years that I've spent in the custody of B.O.P., I've gathered so much hate for the people who helped me get incarcerated that it was unexplainable. I promised myself that before I leave this earth I was going to make them wish that they had took their time like men instead of cooperating like the bitch made niggas they were. It would've been nothing for me to get them hyenas to take care of the situation, but this was personal.

The "Boca-Raton" was the only evidence that the F.E.D's had to kidnap me, and send me away from my family. I wanted to see them niggas die slow in the worst way as possible. After the Boca Raton's cashed me in the judge gave me 8 years and charged it to the game. I hope them rat bastards got their receipts though because I ain't dead yet.

Blew said, "you going to get your peoples to pick you up?"

I said, "I'm going to catch the bus because just my luck I mess around and get locked up riding to B-more, my family would have more than enough time to see me while I'm in the halfway house."

We continued to walk the track until the institutional recall was announced. When I got back to my block, I checked the computer and saw that I had an email from my mother telling me to call home and that it was an emergency. I immediately called her cell phone to see what was wrong.

"hello, Ma what's wrong?"

After a couple of seconds of getting herself together from crying she said,

"they found Little One dead this morning."

I said, "WHAT?!"

I had to act like I didn't hear the words that were coming through the phone on the other end because I was in denial.

She said, "they found him dead this morning Booh"

It felt like somebody just stuck a knife in my heart and continued to twist it and twist it. I felt like I was about to pass out.

Still in shock I asked her,

"where did they find him?"

While trying to calm herself down from crying she said,

"they found him over Eastport . . . in the pool parking lot."

The couple of minutes that I sat on the phone seemed like forever, listening to my mother cry and trying to digest the information that I was just given.

The C.O. came into the phone room and yelled,

"COUNT TIME!"

I tried to tell my mother that I'll call her back after the 4 o'clock count but no words came out of my mouth.

After hanging the phone up, I walked to my cell and thought about Little One. I couldn't believe that my protégé was just murdered, he was my cousin but more like a son to me. I couldn't blame anybody but myself for his murder, because I was the one who introduced him to the Game, when he was only 12 years old. Growing up fatherless like most of the family, I felt as though he deserved to have a shot at the "American Dream." Being that I couldn't be out there to watch him, I made Muse and Black promise me that they'd keep an eye on him.

After count time was over, I called Black's phone to get the whole story about Little One, because I knew the streets was talking.

With a fragile voice, Black said,

"hello"

While trying too keep my voice at a reasonable level,

I said, "what happened?"

Black said, "you know talking on these phones is crazy. I'll let you know everything when you get at the halfway house tomorrow."

I couldn't hold the anger back any longer, I said,

"fuck that! Give me a name."

Black said, "GOD . . . GOD_REALA . . . that nigga Rodney's brother."

I didn't get any sleep that night. All I could think about was Little One and how I was going to make all them Realaz pay at the worst cost.

[This was the first time that I've felt tears drop down my face since long as I could remember. I know in the drug game that it's always a good possibility that you could lose your life or somebody that's close too you could lose theirs. Throughout the whole time I was hustling on the streets, I witnessed niggas getting slumped, but this was the first time I experienced a love one getting killed in a game in which I encouraged him to play. [I was feeling like a paralyzed father watching somebody putting a gun to his only sons head and pulling the trigger over and over. The one thing I did learn while looking back at my life is, no matter how much love you put into the game it ain't going to love you back. Yet it felt good to live the American Dream but look at the outcome of my actions.

When I heard the cell door unlock I opened my eyes and looked at my watch. I must have dosed off for a couple of hours because it was now 6 o'clock in the morning.

The C.O. opened the door and yelled

"WALDERS . . . WALDERS!"

With an attitude, I yelled back,

"YEAH!"

He said, "pack your shit . . . its time for you to get the fuck up out here."

THE END!

ABOUT THE AUTHOR

Jerome Waters Jr. was born in Baltimore, Maryland and grew up in Annapolis, The "Capital of Maryland." After graduating from high school he continued to advance his education by studying psychology at Ashworth Community College and Lincoln Technical Institute.

Jerome Waters is a motivational speaker who hopes to give better understanding and lift spirits of individuals through his words and story. He is at work on his next novel **"CAPITAL OF MARYLAND II . . . BOCA RATON"**

Made in the USA
Lexington, KY
04 January 2013